MW00454162

EVERYTHING YOU NEVER TRIED

Breaking the Rules to Compete and
Succeed Like a Sales Leader

EVERYTHING YOU'VE NEVER TRIED

BREAKING THE RULES TO COMPET
AND SUCCEED LIKE A SALES LEAD

MIKE CARPENTER

I WOULD LIKE TO DEDICATE THE INSPIRATION OF THIS BOOK
TO A FEW OF MY LOVED ONES.

*If we leave a life's legacy, it's that we loved each other well!
My parents, Betty-Jean and Gerald Carpenter, left us too early,
but their lessons on love will last for generations to come. I also
want to thank my children, Grace and Jack Carpenter, for their
enormous love that fuels every part of my existence!*

CONTENTS

PREFACE

FRESH OUT OF COLLEGE, I WAS BEING RECRUITED BY THE TOP five accounting firms, because my accounting GPA showed quite well. Unfortunately, my total GPA was actually kind of bad. I'm fairly certain that the reason for these firms' interest in me was to investigate how this kid with such a low GPA could have an almost perfect accounting score. However, once I landed the interview, I would absolutely kill it, because I was always a pretty solid orator.

Also going for me was that I had my own business since I was twenty years old, and I was making around $50,000 per year while running it. The accounting firms that I interviewed with were offering me between $45,000 and $50,000, and I was thinking seriously about turning them down.

I went home to talk to my parents about the whole situation. My mother was really proud I was going into Boston to meet with these big-name firms. She was of the old-school belief that you needed a certificate of somebody telling you that you could do a job in order to do it right. She wanted me to be a lawyer, doctor, or a CPA—anything that required a license to do business.

She started with, "Are you crazy? Why would you turn them down?"

Trying (unsuccessfully) to reason with her, I answered, "Because they're going to pay me pretty much less than what I'm already making, Mom. I'm an entrepreneur—my own boss—paying myself $50,000 per year. Why would I take this job to sit behind a desk and pour over audit reports all day long? I think I'd hang myself."

Then, my father spoke up, "You know what? I've always wanted to do what you're doing right now. You have your own business, and it's successful." My dad did the books for me, so he knew I was making money. He said, "You're making money, and you're still young. Right now, you have nothing to lose either." Looking at my mom, he explained, "This is the time for him to do this. I always wanted to, but we had too much going on. I had to worry about the kids, college tuition, the house, and all these responsibilities. He doesn't have any of that yet. He's right, why would he take this job? I'm sorry, but it doesn't make any sense."

My mom was furious about the whole situation. She walked out at that point and didn't talk to either one of us for days. Nonetheless, I turned that job down and also took my name out of the running for all the jobs. "I appreciate you guys looking at me," I told them, "but I'm not interested at this time. I'm going to stick with what I'm doing, but thank you for everything."

All's well that ends well, as they say. But, there was one question that stuck with me. During the final interview, one of the partners at the firm said to me, "What do you want to do by the time you're forty years old?"

I was only twenty years old at the time, because I was in college by the time I was seventeen. Regardless of my young age, I was ready for the question and responded accordingly, "By the time I'm forty, which is twenty years from now, I want to be able to retire."

He started laughing at me with that "poor silly kid has no idea what he's talking about" look on his face that adults get when they're about to rain on the parade of the younger generation. He said, "You want to be able to retire? Do you know how much money you have to make between now and the next twenty years to do that?"

Quite confidently, I said, "I know exactly how much I have to make."

With a doubtful smirk, he said, "How much do you think that is?"

I proceeded to tell him how much I had in the bank, and the amount I would need to earn over the next twenty years, or the interest I would need to make retirement an option by the age of forty.

He proclaimed, "You're not going to do that at this job."

"You know, there are a lot of different ways to make money," I responded. "You can have investments in real estate, you can invest in the stock market," and I went on to name a few others.

He said, "You know what? That's true. You've got a good point."

I continued, "I can take my understanding of financials, and leverage it to make personal investments and wise decisions with my money. Just kind of an FYI, but, I may not be here for twenty years."

At that point, I think I won him over, and he just agreed, "No, no, I get that."

We shook hands, and I left even more convinced that I wasn't going to sit there and make $50,000 a year for the next ten years. Also, I wasn't even remotely interested in studying for my CPA night and day, because I hated studying. I was done with that path, and I knew it very early in my career.

INTRODUCTION

MY JOURNEY STARTED AS A "TEMPORARY" VENTURE INTO corporate America. I had spent my early twenties as a successful entrepreneur, running several profitable startups, but as business grew in those companies, I struggled to scale operations accordingly. Knowing that experience is usually the best teacher, I decided to briefly exchange my entrepreneurial endeavors for a job in corporate America that would teach me how to keep things running smoothly post-growth.

At just twenty-five years old, I accepted the role of a young gun as regional director (RD), tasked with turning around the worst performing sales team at McAfee, Inc. in Northern California. One day led to another, and before I knew it, my "temporary" corporate venture turned into 4,748 days (including three leap years)—that's thirteen years, but who's counting?

What happened to the team I took over? More on that in Chapter One, but let's just say that initial success begets more success, and that experience started the ball rolling for me. Opportunity knocks for all of us at one time or another. You just need to be aware enough to hear it when it does.

Since then, I've been named the youngest VP in corporate America at McAfee, I amassed enough wealth to retire by age forty (although I still don't plan on going anywhere for quite a while), and now I'm the president of global sales and field operations at CrowdStrike; the industry leader in cloud-delivered, next-generation endpoint protection.

How did I achieve sustained success? Truthfully, it really wasn't as hard as it sounds. Sure, it required a lot of hard work, more than a few sleepless nights, and some personal sacrifices. But, I did it mostly by taking an unconventional approach to sales leadership, which is easily replicated through the following items of contrasting focus:

- I target growth, rather than covering my own ass like so many ineffective managers did in the past and still do today.

- I value and encourage teamwork and accountability, instead of hoarding individual successes and passing the buck on the occasional, inevitable failure.

- Lastly, I never get mentally exhausted with meeting quotas or toeing the company line with unnecessary administrative tedium. I choose to spend my time more wisely, by balancing flexibility with a smartly prioritized schedule.

One last thing; I took a reasonable risk or two. Okay, one time I put my job on the line (more on that in Chapter Seven), when I firmly believed that I was doing the right thing for the right reason. I sweated that one out until the final hour, but I was young enough to recover if it didn't work out, which was a big reason that I considered the risk to be more "bold" than just flat-out "crazy." That's a fine line sometimes, but I'll show you how that can also be carefully traversed on your way to long-lasting success.

This book will teach you, as a sales professional, how to fight the urge to cover your own ass that is purported by so many of the management clones operating in corporate America today, and forget everything you think you know about sales leadership.

Sustained sales success and leadership requires creativity, a continuous dedication to growth, teamwork, and a few other vital concepts that most salespeople and leaders overlook or dismiss as noble, but unworthy of their time.

Many of the stories you're about to read will include some strong positions—they might even come off as brash and/ or cocky. However, everything we do is colored with intent, and the intent of those written stories can be misinterpreted without fully understanding the proper motivations of the subject, which in this case, is me.

I am an altruistic from my core, and hold an incredibly high regard for treating people with respect. If you understand one thing about me, everything is delivered with an intentional balance of absolute respect for others and a desire to win together. Also, I don't get intimidated or bullied by titles (or by much at all), but I also don't put myself above anyone else.

Every person I engage with is treated with the same level of respect, regardless of their respective title, role, or experience. In turn, I demand that same sentiment to be reciprocated. This is a very strong boundary that I breathe in every day of my life.

My father contracted polio when he was two years old and was one of the final cases in America before the vaccine was established. He spent many of his early days in a hospital, including years in an iron lung. Later on, he attended high school while in a body cast via a hospital bed with intercom systems. Through inner strength and dogged determination, however, he found ways to overcome his obstacles and graduate high school. However, it wasn't without judgment or being told he couldn't be like other kids who weren't as physically challenged. None of his achievements were without sacrifice, embarrassment, and pain.

I learned my abilities to overcome obstacles from my dad, but most importantly, I learned that everyone deserves the same respect. Your shape, color, or any other unique thing that makes you different is what makes you special. That 'special' thing about you can always be turned into a positive in your path of life. My father not only finished school, but he ultimately graduated from college with an MBA. He had two healthy kids, and lives forever in the special things that his experience has taught me through my lifetime. Now, it's my opportunity to help those lessons live on again in you.

With all that in mind, why continue on the path to become just another status-quo management clone? Read on to discover how everything you never tried before can help you to compete and succeed like a true sales leader.

CHAPTER ONE

THE ROAD LESS TRAVELED

WHEN I ORIGINALLY JOINED MCAFEE, THE COMPANY WAS facing SEC issues that claimed overstated revenues and understated losses were reported, and many leaders in the company were, understandably, distracted.

So, authority was delegated to many managers, like myself, which was a good situation for anyone ambitious enough to take advantage of the opportunity. I was one of two or three guys who ran with that delegation, mostly because I was too young to know differently. This began my road less traveled, because unlike most managers in most organizations who are empowered (required) to say, "No," I was empowered (delegated) to say, "Yes."

As a sales leader, the one thing I always wanted to say "yes" to, more than anything else, was growth. Growth is a vital fuel for both organizations and careers to survive, and wherever

I've been, I've always tried to find it, not only for the company I'm working for, but in my own career, as well as the careers of my direct reports.

Growth from a career perspective is usually viewed as the next step. Your next step might be from killer sales rep to manager, or from first-line manager to a knockout sales leader. However, there's an inherent problem with the way the sales industry trains its leaders today, which usually involves the following career trajectory:

1. People get hired as an inside sales rep.

2. They transfer to an outside field rep.

3. The best performers leverage their knowledge and expertise to shoot for a promotion to a first-line manager.

4. First-line managers either stay out of the way to maintain status quo, or become super reps in a half-assed effort to obtain an executive role.

When a strong sales rep is asked if they like their manager, and what it is they like about them, they usually say something like, "Well, they stay out of my way. They deal with corporate, so I don't have to, which is really helpful to me." That means that their manager basically validates proof of life and acts as an intermediary to corporate for them, absorbing a few punches and filtering the non-productive content.

The other traditional role of a first-line manager is that they become a super rep, which is someone who has learned exclusively how to sell over and over again, but not how to lead. It's all about repetition. They've done the same thing for so long that selling is second nature for them. Only breathing is a more involuntary act for this manager.

Leaders Don't Just "Stay out of the Way"

The "stay out of the way" manager leaves their good reps alone, and tries to help their weaker reps make their quotas. That results in their team becoming just like every other team in the organization. Quotas are met but growth is stunted, because there is nothing new going on. This manager is so busy cleaning up their team's administrative tasks that there's no time for creativity, strategic planning, or "outside the box" thinking. It's all been done a thousand times before, and it's how organizations, as a whole, get stale and stop growing. It's also a surefire way for a manager to never stand out or take the next step forward in their career.

A good example of this occurred when I was coming up as an RD with McAfee. During a brainstorming session with all the other RDs in the area, I asked one of them what she thought made her a great manager.

She said, "I do all the shit my reps don't want to do, so they're freed up to get out and sell."

"So, you're basically an admin," I replied.

Slightly offended, she said, "Well, no, I just remember all the stuff I didn't want to do when I was a rep, so I figured somebody's got to do it, and it may as well be me."

I was shocked, because I was unaccustomed to the world of corporate dysfunction at such an early stage of my career. Before McAfee, I was running my own business, which meant I was heavily involved with everything that happened. Such a hands-off approach was like a foreign language to me.

I told her, "No way. You can't allow yourself to be an overpaid admin! You need to come up with strategic plans to help them figure out their territory. They need to draw from your knowledge and expertise about the products, figure out why some of them aren't selling, and change their approach accordingly. Everything needs to be planned."

With a heavy helping of disenchantment, she just sighed and said, "Oh, please. Corporate does all that stuff. They do the pricing, the training, and everything else like that. You just got lucky the past couple of quarters." Now I was the one who should have been offended, but I was too busy looking for another way to beat the average. If you're reading this book, then I'm willing to bet that you're looking for a way to beat the average too.

Leaders Don't Just Become Super Reps

The other typical first-line manager type in sales is the super rep. Most super rep managers never grow out of that role. They know how to sell the hell out of anything, but they never learn how to manage, and they certainly never learn how to lead.

Sales leaders are traditionally hired by promoting the best reps to managers with no leadership training. This sort of development process is akin to taking the best athlete on an NFL team who happens to be a running back, and making him the quarterback. He's not used to calling plays, leading the huddle, and demanding respect and collaboration from the team.

When his team breaks the huddle and the ball gets snapped, he either tries to run all over the field, because that's what he's been doing his whole career, or he tries to throw the ball, because he knows that's what he's supposed to do. Inevitably, he either gets killed trying to run the ball from a position on the field he's not familiar with, or he gets intercepted when trying to throw it, which he has no idea how to do because nobody's ever coached him. Either way, it's organizational chaos.

Fortunately for me, I was hired at McAfee to be a quarterback, not a running back. The best sales rep on the team was the running back. I was brought in to tell him where to run the ball, when to block for me, and when to go out for a pass when I needed him to. I was the leader.

I was running my first business at age nineteen, so I had built different skills from most sales reps who dialed 500 numbers per day and perfected their pitches. My skill set came from going on the hunt for big deals; I couldn't afford to chase down small deals if I wanted to stay in business. Beyond that, I had to learn all aspects of the business—operations, accounting, and everything else.

As it turns out, developing that alternative skill set was critical in allowing me to achieve my success. I missed the boiler room training about perfecting the "don't hang up" sales pitches and jamming the phone lines for prospects and quick closes. Instead, I learned how to hire the right people for the right job, how to give them the tools they needed to succeed, and how to remain relevant in their ongoing success. In other words, I learned how to lead, not just sell. The good news is that even if you came up through the traditional sales channel, you can still learn alternative ways to become a stronger leader and achieve even greater career heights. The inside-out approach described in this book can be implemented at any stage in your career.

Leaders Bring People Together as a Team

I had to confront some very challenging roles along my road less traveled to sales leadership. In fact, none of them were more challenging than the first situation I walked into. McAfee needed a newfound entrepreneur with vision and drive to solve a big problem that had reached a boiling point. That's when I came in.

My mission as RD of that area at just twenty-five years old, was to turn around the worst-performing sales team in the company, which also happened to be located in the company's headquarters. Talk about adding insult to injury. Their insulting injury, however, turned out to be my golden opportunity, and I pounced on it like a lion on the weakest zebra in the herd.

I kicked things off by pulling the team into a nice hotel to introduce myself and I discussed a plan for our team going forward. I told them a little about my background in running my own businesses, and then asked them a little about each of their backgrounds.

After the getting-to-know-you portion was out of the way, I said, "Okay, from what I understand, we have some problems here." Then, I showed them where they ranked with the rest of the company, which was dead last in a lot of categories. I said, "What do you guys think of that?"

They responded, "We think it's bullshit! All of our quotas and metrics are way too friggin' high." They proceeded to rattle off every traditional excuse in the history of sales.

"The product sucks."

"The marketing sucks."

"Everything sucks."

I responded, "Okay, so a lot of things suck. I get that. But if we're going to turn this thing around and become the best, what would you change first?" I got a lot of different responses from that. Some were very valid explanations about why they weren't performing well. Others were just complaints, part of a team-wide bitch session that they probably needed to get off their collective chests. Regardless, we did have to distinguish between the valid reasons and the mere complaints. Whichever category came up, the conversation was still encouraging, because we were getting good information and coming together as a team already.

After we got everything sorted correctly, I said, "Okay, you guys are telling me that if I can change all these things, you could be the best team in the company?"

They responded, "Sure, if you can do all that for us, we can do anything."

"In that case, here's the deal," I said. "There's no way I can get all this done in one quarter (the list was shockingly comprehensive). I'm going to pick one thing every quarter, and I guarantee that if you hit your number, I'll get that one thing changed."

In the beginning, I admittedly chose the low-hanging fruit to change, because I knew I had to put my money where my mouth was if I was going to keep their trust and faith in my ability to make a difference.

Slowly but surely, however, they kept meeting their numbers, and I kept making successful changes. Sure enough, we pulled it off. Like the 1969 New York Mets, we went from worst to first in consecutive years. Luck or skill? You be the judge.

My road less traveled to success has involved some tremendous successes, like that first team I took on at McAfee. It's also included some disappointing failures. For example, you'll read about a whopper—a $10 million one—in Chapter Five. The important thing is that I learned how to embrace both results and learn from them.

Win, lose, or draw, my teams do it together. I take great pride in knowing that I am only part of the team's continuing success, just like I am always part of the team's occasional failure. Along with not just "staying out of the way" and not "becoming super rep," that interpretation of teamwork is key to the inside-out approach to successful sales leadership.

CHAPTER TWO

STOP DOING IT WRONG

ALMOST EVERY SALESPERSON IN THE WORLD UNDERSTANDS that a large part of their success is determined by the size of their W-2. After all, it's bigger than anyone else's in the company. What a lot of salespeople won't publicly admit to, however, is that the size of their W-2 is based almost exclusively on their assigned quota, not a direct product of their kick-ass ability as a salesperson.

All a manager needs to do to prove the link between quota and W-2 size, is tell their best salesperson, "Hey, we're just going to give you a flat percentage on this deal. There's no quota credit involved." Then, they can sit back and watch their best salesperson explode into a hot, frothy mixture of anger and disbelief.

The reason salespeople want that credit applied to their quota is that they want all the recognition and accolades that validate their success to come with it. Different people are motivated by different things, but almost every salesperson I've encountered is motivated very strongly by competition and recognition of success. They want to be able to attend the club events restricted to the high achievers, and to be recognized as a top performer in their industry. Size of the W-2 matters, but quota performance and recognition are equally large parts in the determination of a salesperson's success.

Consequently, leaders should use the importance of recognition to more effectively motivate salespeople. Stop thinking about money as the cure-all for performance, and start thinking more about using equal parts of money, ranking, and recognition as the winning formula for sales success.

Leaders Need to Be Bully-Proof

If you're going to be an effective sales leader today, you need to stop doing a lot of different things the way you've been taught in the past, because they're wrong. One is how we motivate our salespeople, and another is to stop letting top performers or other stakeholders with leverage bully you into ineffective decision-making or a culture of non-growth. Consider the following story as an example of how leaders need to be bully-proof.

I had a rep reporting to me one time who was always rated as one of the top two reps in the company. The problem was that he was also a standoffish, defiant pain in the ass. He was completely non-compliant to every rule I made, and showed up late, if at all, to every team meeting. If we tried to implement a specific strategy, he always voiced his disapproval by saying something like, "What a bunch of bullshit; just go out and sell. It's not that hard."

In just about every review this guy ever had, he got a 4.9 or 5.0 on a scale of one to five, until I came along. On his first review with me, I gave him a 4.0. He responded with, "Can you schedule some time for me?"

I said, "Sure, we can do that."

When we met, he began the conversation with, "I'm the top rep in the company. Why did I get a 4.0?"

"Let's talk about that," I said. "For one thing, you never come to meetings on time. For another, you defy every rule we put in place."

He started to get defensive, "You pay me to sell, not to attend meetings and teach other shitty salespeople how to sell."

"No, I pay you commissions to sell," I explained. "You have a salary as well, and that covers your responsibilities to do the corporate stuff, which is important, and you tend to forget that part of your job."

Switching from defense to offense, he replied, "Look, I need to get out there and sell. I don't have time for all that bullshit you guys keep preaching, because I don't believe in any of it. I just need to go out and make my number. I'm the top rep in the company, and I want a 5.0."

"Let's talk about that," I responded. "Why does it matter to you if you get a 5.0 if all you care about is selling?"

He answered, "It goes into my HR file, that's why."

Then, it was my turn to go on the offensive, so I went on a bit of a roll from there. "I want to explain a couple things to you. The average rep in the company did 55 percent of new business in their patch. You did 30 percent in yours, yet you blew your number out of the water. Why? Because they gave you the wrong quota. I didn't give you that quota, but I've seen how you bully people into giving you a level quota, or you're going to quit. So, they do it. That's not what I'm going to do. The reality is that I don't need you on this team at all. If you think you're that good, and put that much effort into your job, then I'd rather hire two people to replace your ass than put up with this any longer. You're disruptive to my team, and I can't have that going on if I'm going to build any sort of camaraderie around here. You're also a complete asshole every time somebody sits down with you to get some insight into why you're so successful. Therefore, the answer is "no," I'm not giving you a 5.0. In fact, you're lucky I'm giving you a 4.0. You need to change the way you're doing things, because you will never get another quota again without me looking at it first and making sure you're selling new business."

We went back and forth with some various insults and accusations for some time, before it came down to me telling him that he needed to get his shit together and come back to apologize, or get out for good.

He came back after stewing on it for a day and said, "I thought about what you said. I'm sorry, and I'd like to change. Where do we start?"

I replied with excitement to spawn a new chapter in our relationship, after all, this is when true leadership begins.

He ended up completely changing his methods for doing business. Better than that, by reflecting a little, hearing some constructive feedback, and getting pushed to do better, he went on to become a manager, and then VP. He kept his edge the whole time too, but he got a much better understanding that the team is always more important than the individual. Before that, he thought he was going to bully his way through his career, but then he met someone who was bully-proof.

Quota, Schmota

Effective leadership requires some level of being bully-proof. It also requires thinking outside the box of quota, because when managers get singularly focused on quotas, they lose sight of the puck. It's easy to start playing like a bad defenseman and skate to where the puck is, rather than thinking like an All-Star and skating to where the puck is going to be. You should always be planning for the future, but it's extremely difficult to do that if you're always thinking, "Quota! Quota! Quota!"

When I was running the public sector for McAfee, I kept tweaking the business in different directions to stand out. I encouraged my managers to do the same and to constantly push for new business. We did that for some time, and then I realized that if we were going to sustain decent growth, I needed to make a bigger change, so I created an entirely new vertical, which was health care.

The first thing I did within that vertical was to assign a dedicated team to be exclusively focused on it. When reps are focused on selling to a particular vertical, they begin to own their clients' problems and speak to them as if they had the experience to solve them. I also made the patches smaller, and once we implemented those two fairly simple actions, we grew the business in the first year from $13 million to $35 million.

On a more granular level, I had a situation with one rep that fits nicely into this notion that bigger quotas don't always mean bigger success. This rep was very sharp and successful. She had a total of seven or eight accounts, but got very frustrated with me, because I kept shrinking her quota and her patch. Most reps think they need more territory to grow. This case proves that just the opposite (inside-out) is true in some cases.

The reason I kept shrinking her quota was that it allowed her to get into the multiples faster. For example, by giving her a $2 million quota, if she sold $4 million, that meant she hit 200 percent of her plan. Conversely, if I gave her a $4 million quota to start with, she would have needed to sell $8 million to hit the same percentage, which would have been much more difficult, if not impossible to achieve.

At one point, I pulled her into a meeting and said, "You're going to kill me." She asked why, and I said, "Because I'm knocking you down to just one account."

She freaked out, jumped out of her chair, and exclaimed, "That's it, I'm quitting!"

I tried to calm her down, and she was first-class all the way, so she sat down and listened to what I had to say before really unloading on me. I told her, "This account can do $10 million. I can get someone to sell all those other accounts you have if an opportunity comes up. But this account has opportunity written all over it, and you are a great salesperson. So, if you concentrate on this one account, I know you can sell $10 million there, and your number is only $2.5 million. I know you can do this."

Somewhat hesitantly at first, she agreed to my plan, and went on to sell $9 million in her first year with that account. The reality is that most salespeople look at the landscape the wrong way. They think that they need massive territory, numerous accounts, and big quotas. In reality, they might need smaller patches, fewer accounts, and more focus. Furthermore, they need to figure out how they can take less quota with a smaller patch, dig deeper, and trust their skill set to get the most out of that patch.

One caveat to the lesser quota concept is that quotas shouldn't go down on their own without the patch shrinking as well. That's a precarious position to be in, because it likely means that the company is faltering or the business is shrinking. A shrinking quota in the same patch is a sign to start thinking about your next move.

The Good, the Bad, and the Hamburger

Many sales managers evaluate their team, stay out of the way of the top performers, and spend all their valuable time trying to get the bottom feeders to somehow rise to the top. That's a horrific waste of resources. Whenever I took over a team, one of the first things I did was rank everybody, so I knew who my good salespeople were and who my bad ones were.

I didn't want to waste too much time getting to know the bad salespeople, because it was far more valuable to spend time building rapport and relationships with the people who were going to kick some ass for me, not the people who needed me to hold their hands just to get to average. Therefore, I briefly interviewed the bottom-ranked people to find out why they weren't performing.

Some people were failing due to their own fault is what I discovered. They had poor skills, bad time management, lack of drive, etc. Others, however, were failing due to reasons that were completely beyond their control. For instance, they may have had a lot of sales waiting in the pipeline, but the timing just wasn't there yet. Or, they had a lot of activity, but some unforeseen circumstances blew up a couple of key deals. Anything could have happened.

What's important to realize is that I can work with the people who just got unlucky. But, the people who are at the bottom, because of their own ineptness, I let them go right away. I always feel like I'm doing them a favor by helping them to find a career path that doesn't include losing every day. When a career isn't a fit, it's usually not mutually exclusive, and I wanted to help them improve their life. The old saying around McAfee was, "Watch out if Mike invites you over for a hamburger, because he might be helping you find a career you're better suited for."

Sales leadership is almost like a gangster movie in that aspect. As a leader, if you allow a subordinate to stick around who is ineffective or screwing things up for the business, you're perceived as weak. Suddenly, the rest of the team will start to relax and get a little too comfortable. They won't push hard for you anymore, because they don't respect your leadership.

I guess the moral of the story is: don't go for a ride in the Nevada desert with Joe Pesci, and don't go to my house for a hamburger.

Sales Is a Team Sport

From my days as an RD at McAfee to my role at Tanium shortly after that, and all the way up to my current role at CrowdStrike, my greatest successes have always been achieved through teamwork. I'm always confident in my own ability to lead, but sales is definitely a team sport. Think about this: would Phil Jackson have won eleven NBA titles without a great team?

The challenge of most sales organizations is the inherent structure of individualism that exists in the sales role. The emphasis for the sales rep is always on the individual statistics of the quota achievement, and the metrics necessary to produce them (number of calls/day, number of new accounts signed, and number of competitive displacements). The compensation of the sales rep is always tied to these individual achievements through quota achievement, SPIFs, and yearly raises while the manager is the only one held accountable for the team number.

Managers are given responsibility to direct their own patch, but in order to do that most effectively, a collaborative environment must be created from the outset. The team should gather together regularly—without blame—to discuss what's working and what isn't. That meeting should be an exchange of knowledge that benefits everyone. Your job as a leader is to communicate how the team will win together by sharing information. It's a cultural shift from "covering your ass" to "teamwork" where success is not only achieved by all, but increased so careers prosper.

All for One and One for All

The original team I managed at McAfee that went from worst to first serves as a good example of how teamwork can translate to shared success for everyone.

My objective was to turn that team into a group who cared about everybody being successful, not just the individual. Only then, could we actually have the power to request changes.

One of the first things I did was to hire a consultant with a banking background to assemble a penetration matrix, which examines every single territory and shows what products are selling. It also shows where we had success and where our competitors had success. Essentially, we mapped every one of the accounts into what products customers owned from us and what products they owned from competitors. The matrix helped me to leverage my core asset, which was an accounting background, to get the numbers to tell me the story. It revealed trends that showed some reps were really good at selling Product A and other reps were really good at selling Product B. All of these team members had been at the company for at least a few years and were at the point of diminishing returns, selling one product that they were great at.

I asked them, "If you're great at selling Product A, why don't you tell me all the reasons—without blaming the product— why you can't sell Product B?"

Together, we went through the matrix—not the one Keanu Reeves stayed in after he swallowed the blue pill—but the one my banking consultant designed. I worked closely with the group, while sharing my own faults to build up the trust relationship to the point where they felt more comfortable pointing out their own weaknesses.

Change requires a cultural shift, and it can't just be ordered down routinely from the top if it's going to have the necessary impact. Everyone needs a Dave—a person that sets the cultural tone for the team. This person needs to be able to act as the nervous system that fires off the fight-or-flight response for the team. It can't be the manager. The tone-setter has to come from within the team.

Dave was the guy I had to get on board to ensure we weren't rejecting the new organ. In this situation, Dave had an unquenched thirst for creating a science from the "art of selling." He got involved in the planning, took ownership of the matrix, and ultimately was a key ingredient in our efforts to cross the exclusion zone and break ground in territory changes.

I started changing territories based on which reps were good at selling certain products. It was a good way for me to enable people to play to their strengths, but it was only made possible because of the combination of a cultural tone-setter like "Dave" and the prior efforts of laying a foundation of trust that is critical for a culture powered by teamwork. This change was not made easily; within the first thirty days of doing this, I had several people leave or were fired as a result of this approach. This allowed me to rebuild the team around the core values and commitment I was trying to build.

In the past, those people competed with each other, rather than productively interacting. It was all about individual success, which meant there were a few who achieved success, but many more who didn't.

But now the team shared its wins and losses, as well as its success secrets and failures. The reps that hit their numbers and completed their quotas were helping the reps that were still in the fight. Everybody grew a genuine affinity for each other and helped out when they could. For the first time, they leveraged the power of their peers—having clients become reference accounts for others' clients. The more power they had, the more power we had as a team to make positive changes throughout the company.

I leveraged the first few wins with that team to remove some of the smaller obstacles. Every new sale better positioned us in the company with an improved overall performance rating, which opened my ability to make more changes. It fostered an obsessive drive for excellence that drove out the previous concern to cover one's own ass.

That team became one of the tightest units I've ever known. It was the team that everyone at McAfee wanted to join. We supported each other 100 percent, laughing and enjoying our time together the whole way. One team member would always help another if they weren't meeting a number. We even went on trips together. It was a great experience, and it formed some lifelong friendships that still exist today. It's not possible to do that if a few people are going rogue and doing things their own way.

A Perfect Match

When I was named the VP of federal, however, I ran into an outfit with some different challenges that were still closely related to a need for renewed teamwork. My initial call that introduced me to them was met with defiance almost immediately, but it let me know what had to be done to fix the situation.

One of the guys on the team attempted to undress me right away by saying, "Mike, how many years of federal experience do you have?" (knowing very well that the answer was zero).

I replied, "None. How many years of management experience do you have?"

"None," he answered.

Then, I asked him, "How many years of federal experience do you have?"

"Twenty years," he responded a little more boisterously.

Then, I went down the list of team members and asked them all the same questions. They all responded with many years of federal experience, but zero management experience. Finally, I said, "Okay, so between the six of you, there's over one hundred years of federal experience, but I'm the only one with any management experience. Seems like a pretty good match to me."

They all were all shocked by my willingness to extend the olive branch, understand their strengths, and offer my skill set to complement theirs. They all sheepishly responded, "Yeah, well, I guess so."

"All right, now that that's out of the way," I said, "let's get going." Being bully-proof has served me very well over the years in a lot of different situations.

Call Waiting and Waiting

There were two guys on that team, in particular, who were notorious for bucking the system, defying orders, and driving me nuts. They didn't show up for meetings and were pretty damned insulting to some of the other team members. When they got word that I was splitting their patches, they were not happy about it, and they let me know.

One of them was a really old-school sales guy, who went on to become a great executive. He was actually a phenomenal guy, but a little rough around the edges. He had a way of getting under my skin, but now that I can look back on it, that was just a back-and-forth game that we had together. I actually think he taught me more than I taught him through the years!

That guy had the obnoxious habit of picking up the phone, and making the person who called wait for a full five minutes before saying anything. One time that happened when I called him. The whole time he kept me waiting, my blood was boiling, because I had better shit to do than wait for him to finish answering the phone. All of a sudden, I overheard him saying to someone in the background, "Yeah, I was talking to this Carpenter yesterday morning, who doesn't know dick about federal. He thinks he's going to split the territory, but he isn't splitting shit while I'm around."

The whole time he had no idea I was on the other end of the phone, because he hadn't bothered to say hello and find out who was calling him yet. When he finally did, I abruptly reacted, "Why don't you come over to my office to chat for a few minutes?" Click. I hung up and waited for him to show up.

He arrived with his tail firmly tucked between his legs and started with, "There were some things you probably shouldn't have heard a few minutes ago. You should have just hung up when I didn't answer for a while."

I lost it on him, saying, "Fuck that! Just hang up while you're talking shit about me? Not happening!" The meeting lasted a short while after that, but it cleared the air a little bit, and at least I let him know that kind of adversarial bullshit wasn't going to fly with me.

We laughed about that moment years later. He told me, "Man, I thought you were crazy when you said you were splitting the territories, and there were going to be fifteen reps instead of two. Sure enough, by the time you said we'd have fifteen, there were actually eighteen."

The takeaway is that the decisions effective leaders make aren't always the popular ones. Many times, some of the best team members aren't going to get it, and they may not fall in line with it right away. But, you need to find a way to make people understand it, and even if they don't, they still need to get in line with it. Otherwise, it's time to invite them for a hamburger.

CHAPTER THREE

PLANNING FOR SUCCESS

SUCCESS IS LIKE A GAME OF POOL OR CHESS. A POOL SHARK designs every shot to not only sink their targeted ball, but also to set up their next target. Similarly, a chess master will be able to think two, three, or more moves ahead of his opponent to plan an overall strategy to achieve checkmate.

I encourage you to think like a pool shark or a chess master when planning your success as a salesperson. In other words, every move you make should be made with the next move in mind, while thinking as far ahead as possible to overcome obstacles and rise above the rest.

Close Plans

The bird's eye view of the sale is critical to appropriately handling the opportunity. Close plans are account maps that include the following:

- **The coach** – The one who explains what's happening in the business and in the different departments that are influencing the acquisition.

- **The competitors** – Every product from every organization that could possibly act as a replacement solution to the product a rep is trying to promote or sell.

- **The organizational charts of all stakeholders** – Draw an organizational chart of deal approvers, influencers, and buyers to know the appropriate level of authority in a sale.

During closing, reps need to have that visibility of the activity around the sale, both internally and externally. It allows them to make adjustments, convey the message to the right people at the right time, and pay attention to timelines.

As a manager, I think the role is to have the discipline and the involvement not to simply mandate those plans, but to actually walk through the process with reps and help them understand what they need to do. That should give them the ideas they need on how to form a meaningful close plan.

A lot of people demand a solid close plan, but the breakdown in the entire sales culture starts to occur when it's not used. Nobody likes to put paperwork together and then have it collect dust.

Planning separates the good from the great. So, it's important not to rely on soft preparation. Be the pool shark or chess master of sales by planning your territory and preparing your close plans a few steps ahead.

Reps Can Excel with Process, but Leaders Need Flexibility

Reps get pulled in all different directions, and I've seen the ability to keep a tight schedule make a huge difference in success on that level. Once reps advance to management positions, however, disciplines and schedules must adapt for the new needs of the role, because leadership requires flexibility in all aspects of career and personal life.

One of the best reps I ever encountered was a guy named Craig from my time at McAfee. He used to play division one football, and like a lot of the athletes I've seen at an advanced level, he was incredibly regimented about everything, especially his time and schedule. Everything is a simple step-by-step process for those guys, and that ability to coolly section everything off and stick to their calendar is what takes them from good to great.

As a senior rep, he scheduled out every moment of every day, including the time that he was going to spend prospecting. More importantly, he stuck to it.

During his prospecting time, he had a full sheet of who he was going to call, including the content of their last conversation with follow-up items and dates. Prospecting would occupy an entire day, and nobody could reach him when he was doing it.

Craig used the power of process so well that I had him switch verticals several years ago, while he was working for me. He was a top rep in New York selling to the financial vertical, but I moved him to D.C. to sell to the federal government, even though he had no federal experience. (Sound familiar?)

Within his first year there, he won top rep. Now *that* is a testament to the power of process. When we promoted him to manager, however, was when process became a bit of a problem. He took that rigidity regarding his schedule with him to a leadership capacity, which requires more flexibility. The impacts delayed some approvals, missed coaching opportunities, and an overall perception of being difficult to reach. After a few months, I set up a meeting and explained to him, "As a rep, your system works unbelievably well. As a manager, though, you need to open up more time." Craig liked to stay on offense, and answering an unplanned call could alter his game plan.

Today, Craig is a VP of sales, and he learned to adjust his game like all great athletes. He works at a different company, but I still try to call him once in a while. The funny thing is that I still can't get a punch through on the first dial if I'm not part of the schedule. Choose to stay on offense and plan for your success, but don't make your routine so inflexible that it impacts your ability to adapt to the constant changes required in leading people.

Natural Sales Ability ... Who Cares?

When I'm looking for salespeople to join my team, I'll take process over "natural sales ability" anytime. Most people assume that all great salespeople are socially advanced extroverts who are naturally comfortable dealing with people or opening conversations. My experience tells me that's not always true. In fact, some of the best salespeople I've ever worked with are just the opposite; they're introverts.

Sales isn't all about personality or natural ability. It's about process, and I've recognized that the most successful reps have these three things in common:

- **Very high activity levels** – Successful salespeople move one step at a time in very clinical fashion, but they always have a full plate of activity. They make calls and take action decisively without looking back.

- **Highly efficient time schedules** – Their follow-up is second to none, because they keep an extremely efficient calendar. They have all their time blocked off appropriately and don't make a move without double-checking their schedule first.

- **Strong understanding** – They always know what they're selling and the specific value proposition to the customer. The best salespeople also know what their competition is selling, and how to address their weaknesses by extolling the virtues of their own product to solve a particular pain point.

To some, those qualities will come naturally. Others will need to exercise discipline to shape those habits, but I feel like they're within the grasp of most salespeople. If they're not, then that may be a case of someone on the wrong career path.

If you're able to obtain these three qualities—either inherently or through discipline—you will reap the rewards of trusted relationships and happy customers, who are confident that you—their salesperson—will deliver on your promise.

Good salespeople can't be completely void of social skills, however. They still need to have some form of above-average interpersonal communication. Anything more than that, though, may be great in the dating scene, but superfluous to sales. My opinion is that an introverted personality paired with those three criteria associated with activity, scheduling, and understanding will perform as well as any extrovert with "serious game."

Preparation Never Goes Out of Style

An abundance of initial success can lead people to forget all the preparation that got them there. Sometimes, they move off the basics and become a bit lazy about practice and fine-tuning their craft.

The difference between jumping levels in almost anything—whether it's sports, sales, or anything else—is the time you put in. For instance, pop-psych author and noted speaker, Malcolm Gladwell suggests that 10,000 hours of deliberate practice will take anyone to world-class levels in any field. In other words, if you put in enough time and you have an appropriate level skill set, then you become elite. Therefore, if you put in the time to process and qualify the accounts, follow up appropriately, and have a base-level skill set, you will have the opportunity to become an elite salesperson.

There are sales processes like MEDDIC, SPIN Selling, Siebel Sales, and others that some people swear by. Gurus line the shelves in bookstore aisles everywhere with a "revolutionary" approach that's guaranteed to lead to success. The reality is that none of them is significantly better or worse. They're just methodologies, which are fine, but they come and go like the latest boy band on the pop charts. Very few of them work for more than a few years, until the corporate leadership adjusts and a different approach is brought in.

Sustainable growth and success is actually much simpler, because the real work is in the preparation, and that never goes out of style. Invest the time and resources to cover the basics, such as:

- Mapping org charts.

- Understanding the customers' requirements and the ways they're measured.

- Learning what success looks like for the customer.

- Listening to the customers' experience with other vendors.

After the groundwork is laid down, it's time to practice, practice, practice. Start by developing an approach to each customer. Then, develop backup approaches. Plan the direction when the customer says "no" for each qualification process. Every scenario practiced increases the chances of success in future opportunities.

These are the basics of sales that most reps perform somewhat religiously in the beginning, but when they attain success, they veer away from that reliable structure—as if it was for newbies only, but it's not.

Some of the best sales reps and managers I've known, leverage those foundational practices throughout their career. They remain highly active, maintain an almost flawless schedule, have great industry and product knowledge, and continue to execute the basics as well as anyone else.

Danny's Success Story: The Intro

Another kick-ass rep I knew was named Danny. He executed a planning strategy that transferred very well into management roles. As a rep, he spent some time at the beginning of every year reviewing his entire account list. He planned what products he was going to sell to which customers for what dollar amount. He did this for every quarter and forecasted that he would be able to achieve 200 percent of the plan.

Every move he made was planned, including the method, the product, the position, and the opposition (what products the customers already had). He would walk me through it at the beginning of every year. What was most impressive was that Danny's resolve to implement this strategy never waned. He worked for me for several years, and stuck to it as he advanced to a managerial role. To this day, he remains a master planner and is the definition of consistency as a sales manager.

Most people don't have the kind of discipline it takes to plan out such a strategy. The average salesperson usually has a goal number in mind, but they don't visualize the path to success. They just go out and spray their account base willy-nilly without a thoughtful, step-by-step plan.

The appropriate planning represents a logical blueprint for the construction of a successful year. When you know what you need to sell and how much you need to get out of each account, you can start visualizing how it will actually happen.

100 Percent Is Not Enough

Once a clear vision is established, it's time to set goals and add dates to the calendar. With that in mind, it's a good idea to always include a stretch goal in the planning. You should never plan to get to 100 percent of your goal, because that's setting yourself up for failure.

The most successful sales professionals—from the reps, all the way up to VPs plan on a number higher than 100 percent. If the focus is on 100 percent, then the final number is likely to be somewhere around that, perhaps even below it. The common goal for most successful people I know is 200 percent. That way, some actually achieve that 200 percent or more, but most of them exceed at least 100 percent.

Set Quarterly Goals

Setting up a calendar built on a quarterly basis like Danny did, avoids that pitfall where everything closes at the same time, eleven months later. By setting up quarterly goals, your schedule lends itself to smaller, more frequent wins you can use for steady momentum throughout the year.

A good example of this type of strategy in action is how some of the best coaches in college and professional basketball set up a new game plan every five minutes. They implore their team to just play their asses off to win the next five minutes. This tactic has resulted in some of the biggest upsets in the sport.

In sales, we can set up four different ninety-day plans to fill the year. A basketball coach with this strategy might devise a set number of plays to get through each five-minute interval.

When that five-minute interval is complete, the final score is a win or loss. As a result, you aren't waiting the entire game to have a taste of victory.

Breaking success down to bite sizes allows forward momentum to take effect. As a salesperson, however, you need to set up all the required actions, and include the accounts to focus on, and the deals that will get you to where you want to be at the end of each quarter.

A single ninety-day plan won't cut it, though. Properly planned salespeople need to set ninety-day plans to fill the year, so you can clearly see where you're going next. Like the pool shark and the chess master, you're setting yourself up for success.

Categorize Accounts by Strength

It's also critical to categorize accounts based on the strength of the territory—those that are most willing to buy products, down to those still untouched. They always break down into A, B, and C accounts:

- "A" accounts are marked by established relationships. These are accounts that have done business with the salesperson in the past, are open to working with them again, and understand the organization and the buying cycle. Most of your time is best spent here.

- "B" accounts have had limited conversations with the salesperson in the past, but the relationship isn't as strong as the "A" accounts. There is definitely some opportunity here, but you should spend most of your time with these accounts by continuing to develop the relationships first.

- "C" accounts haven't yet been successfully tapped. They require the use of channel partners to assist the salesperson in breaking down any remaining barriers. These accounts shouldn't occupy too much time, because they're not going to produce in the first, second, or even third quarter sometimes. "C" accounts are on cruise control until the trust factor is built, the relationship is established, and a deal can be made that enables you to step on the gas.

Focus on the A-List

The breakdown of accounts into A, B, and C level, also reflects how reps should be allocated. Managers need to keep adding people so that the C accounts become A accounts for somebody. Otherwise, that constitutes an opportunity gap.

For example, if you're running North America and targeting a thousand accounts there, you might realize that 500 of them are on somebody's C list, and the rest are being neglected. That's where you should split territories and invest in bringing in new people and resources. More reps will squeeze more growth out of each individual patch that way. In other words, they'll help to turn C accounts into B and eventually A.

As valuable as it might be to invest proper time and effort into B and C accounts, it's also important to remain focused more on the money that *must* be won without becoming too distracted by money that *could* be won.

Within every quarter there will be accounts that *must* be closed to be successful. Those are the A accounts that have an historical spend with you, and/or a pending need to acquire a product in your space with an imminent event driving the transaction toward a quarterly close. Their presence on the quarter's end will mean the difference between 80 percent of quota and 150 percent. I call them elephant deals, and they require a focused target to figure out how to win the next opportunity within them.

Danny's Success Story: The Conclusion

Danny was the best rep I ever saw at planning his success based on categorizing his accounts. When he began working for me, he was a bit misunderstood. In fact, previous management had him on a performance improvement plan, which is typically the politically correct way of someone telling him that he was going to be fired eventually.

He had a lot of passion, an incredible drive, and a very high activity level. There were also some slightly introverted features about his personality that required patience as his manager. For instance, he really struggled explaining himself sometimes, especially when he got too amped-up to get his message out. Therefore, if I got him too emotional or pushed back on him too much, he would really struggle to orate his ideas, which was extremely unproductive for everybody.

When I enter a new management scenario, the first thing I typically do is I throw away all the history. That way, I'm free to form my own opinion of team members without using feedback from others against them. After interviews, I map their past performance to my impressions to find issues and gaps.

I took an instant liking to Danny as soon as I interviewed him. His exuberance, I noticed, almost seemed like a learning disability that was impacting his confidence. He shifted into self-defense mode too easily, and I thought it would be really good for both of us if I could figure out where that came from.

When talking to Danny, I asked, "Take me through where you think the business is, and how you're going handle it." It turns out that he had an incredible grasp of the business from all the time he had spent mapping his accounts. He was covering the government accounts, and mapped government, IT, and security spend. In addition, he also identified what he thought the patch could do in a given year and where the money would be. So, not only was his planning extraordinary, but his vision was also very clear.

His effort blew me away. Therefore, I figured that I had to find the gap in his communication problems to preserve the abundant resource he had the potential to become.

My first action was to set up several calls with him to try to get to the bottom of things. From those calls, I quickly realized that there was no need for a performance improvement plan, and the last thing I wanted to do was fire him. For anyone that took any time at all to meet with Danny, it was clear to see that a lack of effort was not a problem. His poor performance until that point was purely from a lack of support and confidence.

His prior manager wasn't a manager that went out and sold. He didn't listen very well and he wasn't much of a problem solver. Danny's prior manager wasn't a bad guy, but he just wasn't the right leader for his situation, because he was the very typical example of a "stay-out-of-the-way" manager, who did all the administrative functions to let his team go out and sell. Unfortunately, that wasn't going to get the best out of Danny.

My next step was to personally accompany him to account meetings. I knew I orated very well, so I could cover that gap to get his message across, while demonstrating how to deliver the right messages at the right times.

After spending some time with Danny in the field, he became top rep of the year, and went on to become a vice president. Now, he runs that group. In fact, last year, Danny won VP of the Year at McAfee! That's a long way from the days of his stupendously misappropriated performance improvement plan.

I was flattered to have received a nice message from Danny with a picture of the trophy he got as VP of the Year. He was gracious enough to credit my tutelage as having a significant influence on his own leadership and being partly responsible for his win. We still talk every few weeks, because he continues to value my counsel on his goals, messages, and any issues he's facing. I've always been a big fan of the one-on-one coaching style, preferring it greatly over the "all-hands" meetings that most people sleepwalk, or just plain sleep through. The one-on-one style builds trust and positive relationships that can last a lifetime.

Harnessing Danny's talents to transform his misunderstood communication problems into great results was the by-product of a more hands-on leadership approach. Sometimes, just by being hands-on, you can begin to think outside the box and come up with creative solutions.

Being hands-on can also help you to become more in touch with a lot of things. This type of leadership enables you to not be so blind to anything happening below the penthouse suite. Hands-on leadership keeps vision aligned with the ground floor, which enables better personnel management and streamlined processes as well.

Leaders Streamline Processes

What I learned at McAfee was that as leader of a large organization, it's critical to remember the increased impact of your words and actions, compared to your words as a rep or first-line manager. The messages should be intentional, vetted, and finessed appropriately.

- When you speak or take action as a sales rep, it likely affects only one account or one problem.

- When you speak or take action as a first-line manager, it likely affects the entire team.

- When you speak or take action as an executive leader, it could affect the entire organization.

From this dichotomy, it's easy to see how the effect of your actions increases as your career grows. Most VPs of sales were a sales rep at one point, and when they were, they were very reactionary and tactical. As VP of sales, most keep that edge, so they'll burst out with whatever is on their minds as a solution to a problem without thinking it through. They'll bust out of their office, call everybody's attention, and declare something like, "I want everybody to schedule twelve meetings a week, no exceptions—it's mandatory."

It won't take long for that leader to realize the potential misgivings of their impulsive declaration, because twelve meetings a week may make sense for one territory, but might not for another. How is that leader going to accurately track those twelve meetings a week? Time to bust out that trusty old spreadsheet again, I guess. Maybe they didn't realize the demand on their own time that order was going to have, because now, they'll need to collect and consolidate the meetings that 200 reps are supposed to be scheduling every week. How do they track all that information without inundating themselves and their subordinates with too much administrative time? Being careful with words and actions is a big part of how a leader streamlines processes and plans for success.

CHAPTER FOUR

STOP COVERING YOUR ASS

ONE PERVASIVE CHARACTERISTIC WREAKING STAGNATION ON sales managers is the "cover your ass" (CYA) mentality. CYA managers are afraid that gaps in their business will be exposed. Instead of looking for ways to improve and increase their business, they waste time camouflaging weak spots.

The CYA mentality exchanges progress for survival and continued maintenance of the status quo. For example, consider a manager who has a portfolio of ten products at their disposal with a team that is selling the hell out of two of them, but largely ignoring the rest. That comprises an eight-product gap, which is an obvious weak spot. It's also an obvious opportunity for improvement and increased business for the sales manager with a different mentality, one that is pursuing growth instead of protection.

It's easy to cover gaps like these with standard lip service, which usually involves insulting the product (*never* a good idea) or blaming the message. The reality is that the best products rarely win, but the justifications (i.e., excuses) are virtually limitless in a loss. It's rare that someone actually owns the gap and identifies their personal accountability within it. Conversely, if you take ownership of shortcomings as well as successes, you will have the ability to turn gaps into next-level growth.

Effective leaders will identify issues that fall within their personal control, such as weak areas of business intelligence or insufficient training, and take the necessary steps to make a quantifiable difference in those areas. For example, if you identify a particularly strong pain point in one of your competitors' products, you could then craft a specifically targeted pitch to change the playing field, and lure the customers away. That's the type of growth that can happen when people stop concentrating on covering their ass and look for ways to grow the business.

Closing one gap isn't the end of the line, however. In fact, when one gap closes, another generally opens, because intentional scrutiny finds issues CYA sales managers don't (or won't) identify.

A valuable by-product of owning problems, accepting responsibility, and refusing to blame others is a higher level of respect from the people around you—your peers, superiors,

and even team members in other departments. That kind of positive networking can pay off in unforeseen ways later on.

Break Out of Your Comfort Zone

Back when I was running the federal business, there was a two-person team selling to the Department of Defense (DOD) who didn't want anyone else involved in their business. According to the company's existing metrics at the time, these two reps were considered two of the most successful reps in the entire organization. How they achieved that moniker, however, was by operating entirely within their own comfort zone and keeping all observers at a safe distance. With everyone else out of their way, they could manage their quota, keep expectations reasonable, and limit internal competition.

I recognized that the comfort zone this team had established for themselves would not encourage or even allow for any material growth. After analyzing the numbers, I realized that the best way to instill growth in this unit was to add a lot of people to the territory and split it more strategically. This was a hard decision that wasn't going to make me very popular with two of the best sales reps in the company, but I had to do it anyway.

After listening to me tell them that I was going to add reps to their team, they began their resistance by threatening to quit or make life a virtual hell for me as their leader. Once they realized that I was just fine executing my plan without them if I needed to, and I wasn't susceptible to any bullying tactics,

they provided the following rationale for the status quo: "All of the DOD decisions for security are made centrally. We're covering four accounts: Air Force, Army, Navy, and Marines. Why do we need more than two people for that?"

I responded, "First of all, not all of these accounts buy centrally. The DOD is a global business that reaches across international borders. They make big central acquisitions, but they also have separate budgets and make separate buying decisions. Secondly, we have seventy different products in our portfolio. There's no way two people can appropriately cover seventy products over four accounts." Then, I told them that there would be eighteen people in the DOD business in the next twenty-four months.

Spoiler alert: We actually went beyond my initial projection for reps in that territory. In fact, twenty-four months later, there were over twenty-five people in that territory. To get there, however, was one fight after another with multiple threats from them to quit.

The old saying, "All's well that ends well" held true in this case, because after all the threats, dysfunction, and resistance, they stayed on as integral members of the team and grew with the rest of us. In fact, both of them ultimately became vice presidents in the business and went on to have great careers.

It wasn't easy, but if we hadn't busted down those norms, we'd still have two people selling a slice of the portfolio to

the DOD. The comfort of the status quo is not specific to reps, however. It happens all the way up the org chart, because the industry doesn't inspire people to think of how to grow the business, instill quantifiable change, or become a bigger asset as they become leaders. Too often, salespeople are given reasons to say "no" due to the CYA mentality. Instead, we need to empower salespeople, especially as they move up the food chain, to say "yes."

Become the Easy Win

Based on my observations over the years, the average lifespan of a head of sales seems to be about eighteen months. As these executive turnovers occur from the C-level down, new executives enter and look for easy wins. A good way for you, as a hungry sales rep or first-line manager to take your next career step forward is to make yourself be that easy win.

New executives generally start by meeting with the head of engineering to find out what is working and what isn't. In my case, I'd built a mutual level of trust and performance with engineering, so the answer from that corner was always, "Yeah, Mike Carpenter's work is solid. It would be great to get him into a bigger role, because his team is always figuring out how to solve problems with us."

Without fail, new leadership targeted me for a larger role, because they thought I could make them look good. I was an easy win for them. New executives love to claim an easy win like that, by plucking an internal resource to implement successful change they can hitch their name to. Then, they can bring in a couple of people from the outside whom they've handpicked without anyone complaining, because they've established a history of good personnel decisions already. This strategy may seem like a shortcut, but it's actually good practice. The ultimate winners include the company, new leadership, and of course the leaders that decided to hold themselves accountable for success versus finding someone/something to blame.

A Balancing Act

Things like answering the phone and exclusively dealing with the immediate problem are necessary evils, but it's important to not get bogged down with those tasks. Success is dependent on your ability to handle the occasional discomfort of dealing with those things, but obviously, you need to find time for prospecting and selling more than administration and support. Therefore, the best salespeople know how to handle the ultimate balancing act by identifying the most important use of their time, and planning accordingly.

A lot of the peers I had as a first-line manager spent their entire days playing defense, which is the term I use for handling support issues and problems. This had the effect of turning them all into overpaid assistants, rather than leaders.

Whenever there was a customer problem that needed my attention, I jumped on the phone, pulled support online and made the introductions. I would tell the customer, "I am going to be all over this. We're going to solve this issue, and I'm going to drive this thing to a satisfactory conclusion. Just give me about a week to get it done for you." Then, I would set a calendar invite for three days later to get on a call for fifteen minutes with support and say, "Tell me everything I need to know for when I call the customer back." After that, I could usually call the customer back and verify for them that their problem was indeed solved. If not, I would at least call them back and tell them, "We're still working on it, just give us another few days, and I'll call you back to let you know it's done." Then, I would repeat the same process by checking in with support again a few days later. In most cases, fifteen minutes of my time was all it took for me to get the problem fixed. It's about trust in the system, and trust that everyone will do their job.

The majority of reps and their managers I've seen in my career usually sit on the six-hour debrief and assessment calls with the customer, while they're sitting on the line with support. That's an awfully long time for two valuable team members— the rep and the manager—to be playing defense on a support call, instead of out selling as a rep or planning for more production as a manager.

It may seem like some sort of noble undertaking to best serve the customer, but it's not. It's a gross misuse of resources and a huge disservice to your organization and career. The customer is just as well served, if not better, if the manager doesn't assume the role of admin, and makes a few, quick, spaced-out phone calls to stay on top of the problem, without being out of commission.

I've been in plenty of management meetings where many of my colleagues expressed that they were spending 90 percent of their time on support issues. Meanwhile, I just wasn't having a problem with those things, because I had a different way of handling them.

When the executive leaders asked me, "Mike, are you having the same problem?" I would respond, "Not really."

They followed up with, "You're not having any support issues?"

"No, I've got a lot of support issues," I responded, "but I handle them a little differently. I just tell the customer that I'm all over it, and their problem will get solved. Then, I call support, and get their commitment to handle it. A few days later, I make a couple follow-up calls, and I'm done—problem solved." In other words, I trust the support team to do their job, and I do mine.

All of a sudden, the VPs started saying, "Mike, can you train everybody how to do that?"

It was so easy that I almost felt bad explaining how I did it. All I did was delegate appropriately. I didn't want to spend my time on a support call, because it's not what I'm paid to do. It's what support people are paid to do. Leaders should hold themselves accountable for all the things they can change, not the things that others can change.

I would communicate this to the support people, letting them know, "Hey, I'm going to use this as a relationship boost, so I need to be up to date on everything that's happening. I'm going to let you do what you do best, and I'll check in with you when it's time to contact the customer." They were fine with it and felt a little empowered, because I was giving them authority to handle the situation the best way they knew how.

Transform Problems into Opportunities

As a first-line manager, you can really stand out if you can turn defense (administrative tasks) into offense (sales). From a football analogy, the 1985 Chicago Bears were an historically good defense—so good that they virtually crushed every opponent except one that year who had the unfortunate circumstance of being on their schedule. One of the things that made them great was that they were opportunistic on defense. They were able to score points with turnovers, safeties, and overall dominant play.

We can use this analogy to apply to sales if we understand that a customer's problem isn't always a bad thing, because it could be interpreted as opportunity. In other words, by playing great defense in the handling of a customer problem, we can convert that into points by solving that problem so well that the customer actually wants to buy more from the company.

Eventually, I was able to implement my version of solving support issues company-wide, and it changed the culture in a positive way. It allowed salespeople to sell and support people to support. Of course, there's always going to be some people who don't adapt, and I remember one manager who was laid off. She didn't understand why her long time with the company didn't protect her job, but her success was capping out as she got lost in becoming an admin. (Word to the wise, if you find yourself in this position, overloaded with administrative tasks, request an admin.)

Run, Punt, Pass

When I became a VP, the balancing act to get everything done got increasingly harder, because the problems became harder. To handle those situations that the first and second line managers already whiffed on, I created the run, punt, pass methodology.

- **Run** – This means, hand it off to me, because I'm going to take it to the house! Translation: problem solved.

- **Punt** – Kick it back to the person who gave it to us like it's an anthrax-loaded grenade. We don't want it, because whoever tried to give it to us should have handled it in the first place.

- **Pass** – One of you guys take it. I don't care which, but somebody get open from your schedule for a few minutes, catch the damned ball, and score some points.

My admin, operations leader, and myself classified all of my emails, my recorded notes online, and all of the incoming requests into one list. Every Monday morning, I'd read the list, and assign each item a designation of run, punt, or pass. A list of fifty things took five minutes with that system.

With that process in place, my team would let requesters know, "Yeah, Mike punted that. Sorry, but we're not taking that one." Or, "Yeah, Mike's on this one. You'll get an update from him next Monday." That was the best way of staying efficient and productive without getting too bogged down with the endless line of administrative or support requests.

Don't Waste Time

I filtered the day by items of highest impact for highest return. I wasn't going to do something just because everybody else was doing it. I questioned the precedent if it didn't make sense to me, and I urge others looking for leadership roles to do the same. We should all ask ourselves, "Is this how I should be spending my time?"

One time, McAfee hired an efficiency consultant to see what everybody was doing in the organization. They wanted to make sure that processes were running smoothly and there was no wasted time. That's when I could really stand out, because I wasn't doing any of the non-stop reports and other administrative garbage that nobody was looking at anyway. I don't mind running reports that mean something, but the reports that nobody even looks at are a waste of time, and that's what I told the efficiency consultant. I still remember my interview with him.

He began by asking me, "So ... you don't do any of these things?"

"Nope," I said.

He went on to ask me, "Why not?"

I answered him rather bluntly, "I did them once or twice, and then I realized nobody was checking them, so I stopped, and nobody even noticed until now,"

He pressed on, "You're not afraid to get in trouble for not doing them?"

"No," I responded.

Once again, he asked me "Why not?"

"Look," I said. "They're asking me to do something that doesn't create any value, and they're not looking at any of the output. Why would anybody with half a brain in the organization care enough to punish me?"

That was good enough for them. They stopped their incredulous line of questioning, and I never ran any of those meaningless reports ever again. A leader has to be able to filter the unnecessary tedium out for the team. It's not just about being crusty and saying "no." It's about asking questions and challenging the system to get better. If you throw a monkey on my back in the middle of a race, I am going to ask why, and ensure it makes me faster or its coming right back at ya. As a result, I exempted my team from 80 percent of the stuff everybody else did, which gave them a hell of a lot more time to sell.

Wasted time doesn't just come in the form of administrative tasks or support issues. It can also come in the form of unnecessary meetings. For example, we had an executive at McAfee who was furious one time that teams weren't selling a new product. He got so mad about it that he required every manager to schedule themselves for an 8:00 a.m. call on Saturday morning, or Saturday *mourning* is more like it. Worse yet, the meeting was going to last two hours, where all the area managers would deliver results and plans for change. Who the hell wants to get on a two-hour product call every Saturday morning?

When he first sent out the meeting invite, I declined. So, he sent it out again. The only difference was that this time, he also sent out a reminder to me that the meeting was mandatory. Again, however, I declined.

That's when my manager came running over to me, "Mike, you have to sign up for this. It's mandatory," he said.

I told him, "I'm not signing up for it. I sold all of your new business products, including the one he's pissed about. There's no way I'm getting on a call on a Saturday morning, because that's time for my family. I can understand if I didn't do my job, but I did, so I'm not getting on that call."

"I appreciate that Mike, but what am I supposed to tell my boss? Can't you just get on the call?" he begged me.

I responded, "No. You can tell him to call me, because I would like to explain to him why I will not be attending his Saturday morning call."

"Okay," he said somewhat defeated.

Sure enough, his boss called me the next morning and said, "I understand that you didn't want to be on the Saturday morning review call."

"That's true," I explained to him. "Quite frankly, I think it's a very punitive way to manage people, and I completely disagree with it. If I felt like I had done something wrong, I would get on the call. But I'm your number one leader in selling new products, so I don't think I need to take time away from my family on a Saturday morning for a punishment call on driving new business sales." I was ready to take this one to the mat.

He responded, "Okay, that makes sense to me."

A bit surprised, I said, "So … is that it?"

"Yeah, we're good," he replied. "Thanks for the time, and thanks for explaining why you didn't want to attend." And that was it.

My boss called me back later that day, and asked, "What the hell happened?"

I said, "What do you mean, what happened? He completely understood why I am not getting on that call!" This was as much a lesson for my boss as it was for his. Without challenge or any occasionally necessary push-back, the path to nowhere continues.

Sure, they could have become mad at me, and maybe even held a grudge to make life difficult. It wasn't about me being right and someone being wrong. I wasn't measuring whose muscles were bigger. It was just about standing up for something I believe in.

I don't believe in punitive management actions, especially when it's stopping me from reaching the very same goals they set for me. This should be true for everyone who wants to take that next career step, because we have only so many hands to juggle things with. If it's not productive, don't waste your time with it.

CHAPTER FIVE

BRING IN THE BOSS

REPS WHO WANT TO BECOME MANAGERS, AND MANAGERS who want to become leaders can't do it on their own. They get by with a little help from their friends, which are the engineers, product developers, support personnel, and the boss. Who's the boss? No, it's not Tony Danza, and it's not their manager either. It's the CEO.

From reps, to first-line managers and all the way up, the most important thing about any major transaction is ensuring everyone's fingerprints are on the gun. That way, win, lose, or draw, there are multiple layers of management involved. Everybody can see and understand the painstaking efforts that were taken at multiple levels to enable success, but it just didn't work out.

Accountability is noble, desirable, and admirable, and quite necessary to assume leadership, but the deal might still fail.

Shit happens. When it does, you want to make sure that multiple people down the chain of command have their fingerprints on it. This is symbolic of my methodology, because it's all about teamwork. The team shares in its successes *and* failures alike.

Conversely, everyone appreciates being useful toward a win, so if the deal succeeds as planned, we're feeding the management chain valuable positive sentiments, and that suits the internal politics of any organization very well.

Big deals—career makers—require leveraging everyone's skills that people have access to. Salespeople need to understand that they may have to bring in an engineer to sell a certain product. Sometimes, they may have to bring in support personnel to sell the customer on elite service. Other times, the personal interaction of communicating with the boss may be what's necessary to seal the deal.

This is one lesson that I learned the hard way.

Here's My (CEO's) Number, Call Him Maybe

The story starts with my time as VP at McAfee. I was working very closely with a client, whom I shared a lot of common activities with. We sat on boards, participated in speaking engagements, and even had a radio show that we did together. Although we weren't necessarily personal friends, we shared a great working relationship.

At one point, we were working on a major deal together. In the final throes of the deal, I extended him an invitation to chat over lunch. He was making the decision on whether or not to sign a $10 million deal with us or the competition the next day. So, I took his acceptance of chatting over lunch as a positive sign. At lunch, we talked extensively about our company's offering, our pricing, the testing (which I heard had gone well), and the product in general.

"I understand testing went really well," I said. He agreed and continued to expound on the positive feedback. (My hopes, on a scale from one to ten, officially reached about a seven at this point.)

Attempting to keep the positive momentum going, I elaborated, "Well, you know the price is right and the testing is all systems go. What about your support experience with us?"

He said, "Oh, it's been best in class." (Hopes increased to eight-and-a-half.)

I responded by trying to informally seal the deal, "So, the testing is good, the price is right, and the support is second to none. Is there any reason why you wouldn't choose us to fulfill this order?"

He said, "I can't give you the answer right now, but no. Everything looks great." (Hopes officially at eleven, which to quote the comic genius of the 1984 rock parody movie, *Spinal*

Tap, is one louder than ten. In other words, I was pumped, because it seemed like a done deal.)

I left the lunch feeling pretty good that day, and commenced with high-fiving the reps at the office accordingly. Confidence permeated the air around my team about securing this $10 million deal the next day. Then ...

The next day came, and it went. The sun rose, and it set. No phone call. (Hopes officially back down to around a seven.)

The day after that came, and went. One more sun-up and sun-down occurred. Still no phone call. (Hopes diminishing steadily, right around a four at this point.)

For a couple of weeks, I tried reaching him to no avail, until finally my hopes were officially crushed and reached zero. If I could have taken back any of the premature high-fiving of my reps, I would have.

With seemingly nothing to lose, I left a message on his phone that said, "Hey, listen, we've had a long history of doing business together. You owe me at least a conversation about this. I know calling somebody and giving them bad news isn't the first thing you want to do when you wake up in the morning, but I'm a big boy, and I need to understand what happened. You at least owe me the respect of a phone call."

Two minutes later, the guy called me, "Hey, Mike. You're right, and I'm sorry."

I calmly asked, "What's going on?"

"Well, we went with your competitor," he sheepishly responded.

Frustrated, but not surprised at this point, I appealed for an explanation, "We just had this discussion a couple weeks ago. You were happy with the price. I know we beat them in testing. Why did you decide to go with them?"

"Well, the CEO came to see me, and he gave me his personal cell phone number. It made me feel really comfortable," he answered.

I was glad to have an answer, but I wouldn't say I was satisfied. I said, "So, he gave you his cell phone number ... I would have given you my boss's cell phone. I would have given you a fucking helicopter to his front door if that's what you wanted."

"But you didn't, and your boss never called me," he said.

He was right. I hadn't attempted to leverage the presence of the CEO. I didn't bring in the boss. In hindsight, I probably spent a little too much time getting my hopes up and seeing the reward, rather than recognizing all the necessary steps on the path to success for that deal. That was a hard lesson to swallow—a $10 million one—and believe me, it didn't happen again.

I felt strong about my ability at that time, and I carried a decent title, but what I had failed to realize was that in those mega-transactions, customers want to be paired up with authorities on their level.

This guy was a C-level executive of a major organization, and he wanted to know if the guy at the top of our company was engaged. Even my close relationship with the client and personal recognition in the industry wasn't enough without the visible backing of the boss to close that deal.

These days, I always use everybody in the organization when handling transactions of that size. I love to pair up the CEO, CTO, or CIO—whatever C*O it takes to make the client feel properly recognized. In addition, bringing in the boss tells the client that the business is more robust than one person selling. That crash course in internal politics steered me toward a wider team mentality to include the boss when necessary.

Leaders Form "Big Brain" Relationships

I've always operated with an inside-out approach to sales. Where others valued more territories or more products, I valued smaller-focused patches with higher results. Where others looked to pin poor results on product faults, I looked to address my own weaknesses. I also realized that sometimes my weaknesses called for the expertise of others if my team was going to break down barriers.

My main mantra was always to hold myself and my team more accountable than anybody else in the entire organization. So, if there was a problem, I'd say, "Let's solve it with what we *can* control, and not spend our time thinking about what we *can't* control."

It doesn't do any good to hold other people accountable for performance gaps. A much more successful approach is to introspectively look back at those gaps and expose them to other teams for further collaboration. This sets you up to tackle problem areas with a bigger cumulative brain. For instance, I leveraged marketing to perform studies and communicate with customers to help me figure out how to solve slow growth or address product weaknesses.

The kickback for this kind of bridge building is not small. These "big brain" interdepartmental relationships are highways to valuable inside information. They enable you to change training, anticipate upcoming challenges, and implement a new message (one that isn't handed down from corporate). Before long, peers start to adopt that new message and share the success.

Smart leaders know that sales success and failure isn't always about the product itself, so product blame is not productive. Customers buy messaging. They buy trusted relationships and the attention to detail from the account team. So, while it's easy to point to products or departments to excuse poor sales, the truth is this: most of what sells is within your power, as a leader, to change.

Get Engineering Off the Hook and on the Team

Generally, when I address a rep about a problem with a product, typically the quick answer is, "Yeah, my customers don't like the product. It doesn't have all the features the competitors' products have, and I can't waste my time on things that won't sell."

As I explained previously, blaming the product is just one of many broken tools in the dysfunctional CYA skill set. Inevitably, when that rep becomes a first-line manager, they take the dysfunctional art of product blaming with them. Sometimes, that person holds on to it all the way up to the VP level. It doesn't make them bad people or even bad employees, but they just never learned how to redirect their focus to improvement over covering their own ass.

Blaming the product at the VP level will only serve to burn bridges with engineering and other valuable stakeholders, which is a growth killer. Sales needs engineers on board to meet requests for feature enhancements and product improvements. If the two sides are constantly butting heads or pointing fingers, rather than collaborating or innovating, business never grows, the customer never wins, and neither does the savvy sales leader.

Ditching the CYA mentality means an end to that transfer of blame and restoration of critical interdepartmental relationships. Opportunities are no longer reduced to dead-ends, pitting department against department. The absence of blame alone goes far to build trust—especially with engineering, since they're usually the group bearing blame for a product that supposedly can't sell.

When engineering believes sales is on their side and the two departments support each other to build new features and products that meet customers' needs, business grows and everybody wins. I've even seen engineering voluntarily interface with customers on sales' behalf. That's the kind of game-changing relationship that you need to foster as a successful sales leader.

Transparency Creates Opportunity

Earlier in my career, as first-line manager, I was working with this state and local government education group near New York, running the Eastern U.S. territory from the New York City office. While working on a couple of critical deals, I reached out to the president of the business unit and said, "Hey, when are you coming to New York? I want to get you out in front of a couple of our key customers."

When I shared this in my team meeting, my sales guys said, "Are you crazy? We don't want him in our meetings. He'll be all over us. What happens if it doesn't go well?"

We discussed it a bit more, and after reflection, I said, "Guys, we need to involve the executives in the business to show them what we're doing. There's no reason to fear anything.

We put in our best effort every time, and generally do things the right way. Don't you want them to understand what we're doing and why we're being so successful?"

The risk still felt too high for them. To try to put them at ease, I committed to attending the sales calls with them. We planned to start strong by meeting with customers we knew really well.

Finally, the president accepted my invitation, and I took the opportunity to illustrate precisely how sales transactions happen. I also explained to him how a shift in the comp plan from the C-level removed our leverage with customers by not paying the reps on renewals.

I said, "They're no longer working on the transaction. Our ability to wrap and roll, and add new products to leverage for the imminent event is gone." Then, I introduced him to customers who had experienced the leverage we once had, so he could see the difference.

It was a good example of what happens when a leader just acts without giving his idea the proper consideration and planning. He just figured renewals were going to come in on their own. We have a 90 percent renewal rate. Why are we paying people for it?

He didn't realize that renewals created an imminent event, which served as incentive for the customer to be involved with us. Indirectly, it gave us another opportunity to grow

EVERYTHING YOU NEVER TRIED

and add a bunch of new products. So, when he dropped that from the comp plan, people stopped working on renewals. Consequently, our business started to tank.

He had no idea why business was tanking until he saw first-hand a view of the power of that transaction. When he left, he changed the entire go-to-market model for the organization. He changed to a model that was better from the sales rep's perspective, which gave us just about every resource we could possibly need to be successful.

The customers were also impressed that the president was in tune with the business enough to visit state and local customers. The outcome across the board was incredibly strong, although the reps hadn't initially foreseen the power that the transparency of their work could provide.

Danny—for one—couldn't believe how well that open invitation to the president worked. That visit worked out so well, that it launched a revolving door to my region from the entire new executive team. They each met the reps, saw what they did, personally witnessed their drive, and acknowledged how they treated the customer.

Reps play at a disadvantage when they insist on meeting with clients alone. They may be able to run the smaller deals, control all the pieces, and have numerous individual victories, but those are what I call W-2 victories. If reps want to grow in an organization, they need to show up for judgment day. That means letting people see what they're doing, allowing others to see how they're different.

Transparency with management about your ability to change the organization will advance you as a leader.

When and Why to Invite Management

Recognize that upper management wants to be a part of the sales cycle. Determine which members of upper management belong on the team by the size of the deal and their ability to make a difference for the customer. In the FAA deal, for example, bringing in the boss would have made all the difference. It was a big enough deal, and it would have flat-out closed it.

You certainly don't need to bring the CEO in on every deal. Look at the average sale price. If it's $100,000, it means that probably 10 percent of the transactions are over a million dollars. Those are the deals to leverage the power of the CEO. It will be different for every organization, but generally, about 10 percent of sales will benefit from that top-level involvement.

First-line managers are pretty much mandatory to include in any deal of note, because, they're usually the best rep in the group. So, getting their third-party assessment or guidance is usually an intelligent first step.

The second line of management—VP levels—can afford you access to high-priority resources. They can provide special pricing approval, access to a better delivery person, product changes, and other things that may provide value in convincing a customer to do business with you.

Bring in Support for ... Support

That's essentially the way to navigate straight-line (north-south) management, but there's value in going wide (east-west), as well. Most people in support roles also play a critical piece in the food chain of organizational long-term success, yet receive little recognition. These mostly unsung heroes don't travel, and they deal almost exclusively with pissed-off customers without sharing in the victory of a win. If you're a sales rep, this should spell opportunity for you.

Bring the support team into the very beginning of a deal. It takes a lot of empathy and strength to be in that role, and that will carry over to the customer. Customers will see who they'll be dealing with when problems arise, which is incredibly powerful in terms of relational trust. A side benefit, of course, is preferential treatment. I had support problems get bumped up in urgency because my customers and I had such a great relationship with support personnel.

Get Finance Involved

Now, as the president of the business, I bring in my CFO to explain to customers how we're measured by investors and by the street. I get the customer to buy into their interest in my success. They understand that the more money the company makes, the more we put into R&D. For them, it's a direct correlation to value and security.

When my CFO helps explain to the customer how the company is valued, it paves the way for me to talk to them about the price point and the reasoning behind the pricing structure. I explain discount levels and why we can't drop that price. All of this talk loses the stigma of "sales speak," because it's stamped with the endorsement of the CFO. It's even more powerful when you have a CFO who really understands the business beyond the numbers. I have been very fortunate at CrowdStrike to finally meet one of the best CFOs in the business. I take Burt into every mega opportunity I have. Most people never include their CFO in the pricing discussions, which limits their flexibility, and does nothing to remove the sales speak from the relationship.

What happens when I need to go a little bit lower on price? I have the CFO sit on the call. They hear the problems and all of my efforts to hold the margin at a certain level. This invites them into my victories, and assigns to them a direct role in the best part of business, which is the revenue. The outcome is this: If I need resources, I get them, and if I lose the deal, I have the CFO's fingerprints on the gun. Imagine the value of the CFO saying, "Hey listen, I was involved with that one. That guy did everything he could to win. We just didn't have it."

How to Prepare the Management Team

When the deal is big enough and the value of bringing in upper management to the deal is evident, make sure they're properly prepared. Use the deal sheet to expose weaknesses and gaps where the company leader would have greatest impact. Follow these general steps to appropriately welcome top-level management on board.

1. **Create a concise one-page internal document** for the leader that includes the following:

    a. **Customer org structure** – Who will management be talking to, and what do those people control?

    b. **Deal criteria** – What is the business, and how do they make money?

    c. **Areas of wins and losses** – What does the customer win by buying the product. Where do competitors score points?

    d. **Desired outcome** – Describe the projected impact of this management leader.

2. **Hold a fifteen-minute phone call** to lay out precisely what is needed from upper management.

3. **Thank the leaders for their involvement.** Fuel their future motivations by letting them know how using their authority to assist in this deal is immensely appreciated, because it will serve to further the organization's mission.

A tight prep sheet will properly equip management to hit the ground running with focused intention and the best odds of achieving desired outcomes.

As leaders advance, the opportunity to be in on the ground floor for wins diminishes. There are fewer chances for individual success. The issues they encounter are harder, because quick wins are usually claimed earlier in the process. Problems at this stage are ridiculously involved, and the solvable portion of them (since some are not solvable) will usually take a minimum of six months. So, the high concentration of small wins that reps enjoy offers a tangible currency that reps can share with the top of the food chain.

CHAPTER SIX

MORE THAN SUCCESS

SUCCESS IN MANY PROFESSIONS AND ENDEAVORS IS SEEN AS progression. For instance, if a weightlifter lifts one hundred pounds today, his next goal might be to lift 125 pounds tomorrow. Sales reps are no different. They want the next goal, and for most of them, that's management.

Most reps measure success in the short term on a W-2, but leaders look at it differently. As a leader, success is contingent upon the ability to help other people succeed. It's a necessary transition reps need to make when they become leaders, because there's a huge difference between winning for the individual and winning for other people.

An individual contributor is mostly concerned with their own success, and their personal measurement for that is usually direct compensation. But making quota isn't the same as leading. In fact, being a manager isn't necessarily leading either. Just think about where the root words to *manage* and *lead* come from.

Managers Manage, Leaders Lead

To *manage* is to manipulate, control, or provide administration of something or someone.

To *lead* is to pave the way for the achievement of a team in the pursuit of a common goal. It's to measure oneself on the ability to make a change in somebody else's life for the better.

Those who don't understand that distinction and know how to enact it appropriately, are done at level one. They're not going to be able to make that leap from rep to leader effectively, and there's nothing wrong with that. There are plenty of sales reps that rake in eye-popping W-2s for an entire career, and set themselves up for a nice life with a comfortable retirement.

Leaders, however, understand that distinction very well, and they enjoy building, architecting, and designing things. Reps who combine this understanding with a plan for their career path to leadership—a plan that is as diligently created as their sales strategy, will set themselves up for more success.

Reps or managers who want to take that next career step to being a leader, need to start thinking in terms of being a thinker. Instead of performing the same sales routine over and over again to meet quotas, thinkers need to start developing a different skill set—one that involves observation and analytics, more than sell, sell, sell.

Watching the way in which a person performs a particular action, analyzing it, and adding insight to help them do it better was always so fulfilling for me. I never want to take it over and do it myself, but I have always liked the coaching aspect of my job.

Observation and analysis were two tools in my skill set that probably came from my participation in sports when I was younger, and I think they've served me quite well. I spent a lot of time watching film, because I had the ability to identify the little things people did that gave away the play. Occasionally, I would glimpse a player's "tell," like an involuntary turn of his hand before he hiked the ball. Something like that could enable the entire defense to jump the snap count and get consistent pressure on the opposing team's quarterback. Anytime I caught something that could help the rest of the team, I showed everyone else what I saw, so they could read the game better, too. My predictions weren't always correct, but to me, an observational discernment was my talent and something I always enjoyed doing.

Career Evolution

Managers will make less money in the short term than the best rep, because they're paid based on the total performance of their reps. As with any profession, some of those reps will be great, but others will fall into the "not-so-great" category.

Naturally, the income as a first-line manager will be less, but in off-quarters, the income maintains a relative stability. Not every rep on the team will miss at the same time.

The long-term play for most managers is to continue rising, because the money is made in equity—not commissions. Equity comes from a manager's relevance to the organization. Generally, a manager will gain increasing amounts of equity with each step up the chain of command.

I've met some managers who are built to be the player coach. They like the closer interaction with the team members, and they love being on the ground floor of where the action is. Therefore, that's where they want to stop—at first-line manager—because the higher a manager goes up the ladder, the further they get from the transaction, and that's not where they want to be. It's rare in my experience that someone wants to stop there, just like it's rare for a rep *not* to want to get into management, but it happens.

The more common desire for most professionals—whether in sales or almost any other career—is to evolve. We're naturally wired that way, and society is structured to provide the environment necessary for us to do it.

As children, we go from first grade to second and so on. In first grade, we learn the fundamentals of reading, writing, and mathematics. Then, in second grade, we're taught the lessons necessary to further develop those skills, and our ability in those areas and others advances with each subsequent grade. Thus, we evolve our intelligence and ability to contribute to society.

Likewise, when we become adults, our careers should take a similar path. The first company we start with should allow us the opportunity to develop a skill set. Every so often after that, we should take the necessary steps in our career to further develop that skill set. When the company we're working at doesn't continue to evolve its business, it may be time to part ways. Otherwise, we get stuck in a stagnant career with a company that's not growing with us. Beware of the company that stops growing, as it's the first sign of a need for change.

Reps Beware of the Decreasing Quota

When I was first-line manager at McAfee, there was a mixed group of about ten of us—reps and other managers—who would pitch in on a big house to go skiing in Tahoe for long weekends together. Some of us worked at McAfee and others worked for other companies. One of the guys from a different company was always bragging that after he got his quota, it would go down. He'd spend the whole ride up talking about this.

Everyone was so jealous. They said, "Man, you're so lucky! My quota always goes up."

Finally, one of the guys near me leaned over and said, "Man, his quota always goes down. How come he gets so lucky all the time?"

"Oh, no, you're looking at it all wrong, my friend," I told him. "If his quota is going down, and his territory is getting bigger, not smaller, that means his company is going out of business. He will be looking for a new job within a year."

Within a year, the guy's company was sold off for parts like an old American muscle car, and he lost his job. Unfortunately, that event had a career-changing effect on that guy's future. As a leader, it's important to identify the signs of a sinking ship, because being noble and riding the Titanic down to the bottom of the ocean has no place in career growth. In hindsight, a mindset geared toward evolution and growth, rather than the routine of selling products and meeting quotas, would have been a very valuable skill to have.

All Good Things Must Come to an End

Every role in business has a finite cap when there's no more growth left. For instance, a rep who already earns $200,000 to $300,000 a year should be able to win the majority of buyers and be sold out within three years. That finite cap is there for each role as they move up the corporate ladder.

If you stay in a position too long, the capacity for continued success diminishes. You should be thinking about changing roles approximately every three years, or you'll stagnate and experience a drop in earning potential. From a management perspective, if we can't make change that merited an advancement in the first three years, what's going to change in the next three?

To sustain career growth, it's critical to keep moving forward, and take on new challenges, but sometimes the company doesn't offer them. Their corporate culture may not be one that encourages growth. Companies like that may lack an innovation mindset and that will hold you back.

For example, Intel has a ten-year roadmap. When they purchased McAfee, they requested a ten-year plan from us, but McAfee is a software company, and software companies don't have ten-year plans. With the constant change of the software landscape, we're lucky to have a three-year plan. Outside of general ideas, software companies can't plan out much further than thirty-six months. Hardware, however, is highly calculated and planned. They know a majority of the features they want to build into a given chip ten years in advance.

Those disparities in plan don't necessarily hold a growth-minded salesperson back on their own. Career evolution doesn't depend solely on the company's ten-year plan. However, setbacks occur when companies say they need to keep people in certain roles, because they're so great at them. That's the kind of business decision that shortsighted leadership makes. They think only of their immediate, individual interests, rather than promoting the best interests of everyone involved, which will pay long-term dividends for the entire organization. If you find yourself mired in a situation of cultural dysfunction like that, move on before it's too late.

The flip side of that coin is a company that thrives on innovation, fosters growth, and powers forward to continuously evolve. Salespeople who are fortunate enough (or diligent enough in their selection process) to find themselves working for a company like this, still have a few knobs to turn on their career machine to continue their own evolution. These knobs are labeled territory, quota, and product.

If the company is truly in a constant cycle of innovation (e.g., Apple, Amazon, Tesla), then it's easy enough to just add a new product. Without new products, however, something else has to change. This is when you need to switch patches, seek a promotion, or switch companies.

In terms of quota, it doesn't necessarily need to be bigger—just different. Quotas and patches are tied together, so if one element changes, everything changes. For example, a rep's quota could remain the same in the midst of company growth, which means the patch would decrease. Essentially, that means you're drilling down into that smaller patch to bring B and C accounts up to A accounts with more vested time.

Change can take place in more ways than one, but it must show its face every few years if growth is to persist. It's a concept that takes most of us outside our comfort zone, but how else can we grow? If all we ever do is whatever feels comfortable, most of us would never get off the couch with the warm, electric glow of the television set numbing our brains to complete inactivity, as one day melts into the next with no accomplishment, no growth, and no evolution.

Identify and Create X-Factors

To ensure I stepped out of my own comfort zone every so often, I created some X-factors to nudge myself further and measure my own success. X-factors are things within our control that we can do personally to make a difference. They consist of small stretch goals like a ninety-day push goal that's more than a simple quota or number of buyers. It's a good way to periodically assess the difference you're making for the team and the company.

Some good examples of X-factors would be allowing ninety days to find a customer who will take a product for free in exchange for participation in a live product demo, or getting 125 meetings to come from your venture capital team.

I customized my own X-factors to meet my personal expectations for growth and reviewed for change whenever they were finished. Sometimes, the timeframe of the X-factor was six months. Other times, it was ninety days, depending on the scope of the change that needed to take place.

When I felt like we needed to activate our negotiations to grow revenue, I focused on team development in that area, measured by the team's use of discounts. Clearly, discounts are one of the fastest ways to speed negotiations, but I saw opportunity for growth there as well. Instead of leveraging the quick tools, I brought in negotiation trainers and personally engaged in deals, so salespeople could carve out new paths to deals. The goal was to lean less on a tool, and it worked. A few months later, the team had the muscle memory for stronger negotiations.

Future leaders set challenging X-factors. Even if you fail to reach 90 percent of them, you still know you're innovating. After all, the innovation that comes out of 10 percent of pre-set X-factors is better than zero innovation coming from zero X-factors. Allowing for that much failure goes against a CYA impulse, but it's the most effective way to create space for growth. If you're always achieving your goals, that also means that you never know how much more you could have achieved. It might seem counterintuitive to think of failure as growth, but it's symbolic of my message in this book. It's a great way of trying something you've never tried before to compete and succeed like a true sales leader.

One of my most successful X-factors was sending free, new products to new accounts. During a time when McAfee was making a lot of acquisitions, I knew that if I could get on that acquisition team, I could find out a ton of great information about the products we would be selling from the transaction. So, I made a lot of requests to all the right people, and ultimately succeeded in securing a place on the acquisition team.

Once I got there, I gained so much preliminary information that I became an internal expert on the new business. I already knew about the new product, the customers, and everything else I needed to set my team up for success.

I was prohibited from sharing information before the acquisition closed, but I was permitted to prepare a game plan that would allow me to take incoming products to market faster than anyone else. There were rules in place that limited what I could do, but I followed my mantra: I did what was within my control.

Eventually, I set a goal to incorporate the new product into about 80 percent of our transactions. My overall plan was to wrap and roll the new product into negotiations according to the game plan I set up.

By the day of closing the acquisition, I had planned the pricing discounts my local team would utilize, and I assembled all the accompanying marketing material—messaging, pricing, and appropriate branding. Equipped with a list of all the upcoming renewals, I flew in my team and took them through the entire go-to-market plan. We seeded the whole area with specific products at specific prices. They had everything they needed to sell right away, and that quarter we sold more in my team of six, than the entire global sales organization, and it all started with a simple X-factor.

Where to Go from the Top

What happens when you reach the pinnacle of your role, and you've already been there for more than three years? That's when you need a plan, and you need to act on it.

1. Top leadership needs to know when you're ready for the next step in your career evolution.

   a. There are always discussions—formal and informal—about new opportunities for advancement and who should be considered for them. You need to make sure that your name is thrown around in those discussions. Sharing your timeline for growth and career goals is one way to make sure that happens.

   b. You can't be shy about adding your name to the list when the discussion of advancement opportunities is being had. Announce your own timeline and goals loud and clear, while also stating the future value you can add beyond your current capacity.

   c. Be likable. Nobody will volunteer to manage someone they don't like, and they certainly won't nominate them for advancement if you're argumentative or have a competing agenda.

2. Make sure you're successful in your current role before striving for the next-level opportunity. Timing is everything, and if you're perceived to always be looking ahead, rather than first achieving success in the present, you'll never be taken seriously for anything bigger.

a. The current plan and quota should be hit and surpassed. After all, nobody says, "Hey, this guy always hits 60 percent of his plan. Let's give him a bigger role."

b. Strike while the iron is hot. You can't wait until a cool-down period hits. Again, timing is everything, so the time to strike is when you've blown away your number or have been recognized as creating something special.

CHAPTER SEVEN

MANAGER MATERIAL

THE MANAGERS WHO BECOME AMAZING ARE FEW AND FAR between—about 5 percent in my experience—and it's because they lead. They don't simply "stay out of the way" or continue to be the "super rep."

The Five-Percenters

Amazing managers aren't magicians. They don't use slight of hand to create the illusion of success. The five-percenters who become great managers grab the reins of leadership as if they're the CEO of the company, and immediately start questioning, analyzing, and planning.

- First, they assess the talent on their team and question whether they have the right people in the right roles or not.

- They analyze their territories to see which ones to quit and which ones to split.

- The five-percenters think about ways to squeeze more growth out of the business, so they plan to be 200 percent of quota.

- Great managers immediately look for the X-factors that might benefit everybody, not just the individual.

- They look for blind spots of their own, on the team, and in the business. Then, they seek to understand them and rectify them internally for optimal transparency.

- And, they leverage their strong suits for the team to bolster everyone's sustained success.

Ego Grows with the Leader

Every individual's career has the opportunity to take right and wrong turns. Ego plays a major role in that.

In order for your career to grow, your ego has to grow with your career. You need to believe in your expanding set of capabilities. After all, the ego protects you as you go higher up the chain of command. But the ego can also lead to problems. An overgrown ego can corrupt you based on the power you've amassed.

Think about the NBA finals and all the trash talking they do. Watch all that rhetoric surrounding the big MMA fights. It's not just marketing. These people are building their own internal confidence and ego, while trying to crush similar traits in their opponents. They're convincing themselves, their opponent, and the world that they're unstoppable. True, they may not win, but they refuse to enter already defeated.

In business, there are fine lines. It's possible to cross the line with too much confidence, and then you just look ridiculous. There's a fine line between confident and cocky. Confidence exudes trust and dependability. Cockiness exudes annoyance and resistance. It's important to check yourself constantly to know if you should pull back temporarily or continue to push forward.

Confidence will be the most common conflict an executive has. As you gain your sea legs in big business roles, you need to simultaneously build your confidence to deal with the escalating responsibilities. Equally important, however, is that you prepare to pull yourself back into an ethical and moral foundation when necessary.

An Ego Run Amok

I remember one CEO who was heavily trying to recruit me to be president of the Americas. We had been talking and working out details for months. One night, we went to dinner. This guy had the polish—replete with a confident swagger and a well-rounded and experienced background. When it was time for dinner, his food didn't come out exactly the way he had requested.

It's fine to be disappointed in a meal and send it back, but this was something altogether different. This guy pulled rank with phrases like, "I know the owner" and utterly destroyed the server in a public display of personal ridicule over it. The whole scene was completely unnecessary and extremely embarrassing.

Right away, red alerts went off for me. While I felt really bad for the poor server who was the subject of his scolding, I also began to relate the situation to what it might be like to work for a guy like that. I knew then and there that this was not a man I could trust. Truthfully, he didn't seem psychologically stable from the way he acted that night.

Later on, when I returned home from dinner, I called the chairman—a friend of mine—and said, "I'm going to turn down the job."

He asked me why, and I said, "Listen, I know it's going to sound crazy, but my personal mantra is that I treat everybody the same way—from the janitor to the CEO. I just can't deal with someone who would humiliate another adult in public. If they'll do it to someone over a meal, they'll eventually try the same bullshit with me."

Later, the company discovered that this guy, who had been

heavily engaged in the process of purchasing $500 pens to give out, had been keeping them for himself. At the same time, he would seize the opportunity to make himself feel superior by making fun of the pens other executives were using. He did the same thing with custom shirts, and ordered spa certificates to distribute to his girlfriend. To me, this guy oozed volatility from the outset, and I was fortunate to have avoided him. Within a year after our meeting, he was fired for a mixed bag of issues that all come back to an ego run amok.

Change Is Opportunity

There's something about human nature that repels at the thought of change. Most of us get complacent, and when the winds of change start blowing through, the natural reaction is to defend. But, that is categorically the wrong way to look at change. Rather than putting up defenses, you should look at change as opportunity.

Leadership changes are inevitable. That's okay though, because change is a chance for a clean slate. Even though I was never terribly fearful of change, I knew that a lot of people on my team would be, and part of my job was to settle them down and offer some stability.

I would tell them something like, "Now's your chance to reflect. You have a clean slate. Any commitments you made or anything that didn't work—they need to go. Put it all behind you and try again. Go educate somebody new in the business. Get to them first and bring them into our patch."

Changeover to new leadership is just another opportunity to get someone with some pull—some real value—on the team. One caveat: It's important to recognize a person's strengths and weaknesses at all levels of the organization. Some top executives are great at some things, but not so great at others. For example, I had some executives who weren't great at selling, so I'd only take them to people who I knew wouldn't hold it against us.

Identify Strengths and Weaknesses

There was a CEO I worked for once who didn't know the products very well, so he would talk about it as "stuff," and it used to drive me absolutely nuts. To hear him talk about our state-of-the-art product line as "stuff" was like fingers on the chalkboard to me. As it turns out, technical aptitude just wasn't his best quality. He couldn't properly orate any of the advantages of the product, so he just routinely touted, "We've got great stuff!"

In a respectful and professional manor, I tried to coach him up a little. "Hey, would you mind not calling the product, "stuff?" I know it sounds good to you, but I don't think it puts our best foot forward." Then, I tried to brief him: "Here's the product name. Just talk about the fact that it has great future releases planned, and you're proud of the new platform."

Ever play a pickup game of basketball at an outdoor court with the sun beating down on everyone, and the teams were comprised of "shirts" and "skins?" Inevitably, there was always one guy on the "skins," team who sweated just by thinking about playing sports. Whoever was unfortunate enough to try to guard him would get a heavy dose of perspiration splattered against them every time they made contact. That was this guy. He'd shake someone's hand, and they'd wipe it off on their pants at the first chance they got when he wasn't looking. Spotting this as a hidden weakness, I was always careful not to take him out to customers on a hot day. Instead, I'd keep him inside his air-conditioned office on those days, and bring the customers to him.

The flip side of the coin with this CEO was that he was very good at certain things. He had a big personality, which could definitely be used as a strength. He had a great way of bringing people together, especially when he was teamed up with other big personalities. He always got along really well with ex-college athletes and extroverted types, and he had a knack for getting a lot out of them.

Sure, he had some weaknesses, but he also had some tremendous strengths, and the key was just knowing how to leverage the right things. It would have been easier—with all the coaching required—to bypass him completely, but the hard work paid off. In the end, he felt useful and got to use his strengths to provide value, while I leveraged the power of his status and his big personality to sell to the right customers. It was a win-win, and it always is when people are empowered to play to their strengths.

Recognize What Makes Someone Special

Throughout my career, I've always tried to maintain a good awareness of what I had that was special and unique, because I wanted to expose it for everyone to see, and leverage it in any way to help the team win.

Many of the qualities I've used to my advantage in my life came from my upbringing. When I was a kid, I learned early on about some very powerful lessons like hard work, perseverance, and how to embrace change and battle adversity.

My dad had polio from the time he was two years old, and I always had a tremendous amount of admiration and respect for the way he handled it.

He spent his high school years in a body cast and lived in an iron lung for an extended period. As he grew, he had stomach braces to hold the stomach muscles in. Throughout a majority of his childhood he spent a lot of time in a polio hospital—quarantined from the family or recovering from a surgery. Eventually, he was on crutches and in a wheelchair toward the end of his life.

He clearly had a severe disability, but not once did he talk about it. Not once did he take a government subsidy for the condition. Occasionally, people would ask him, "What happened to your foot?" Usually, he would just make up a story that he had broken his ankle somehow.

His disability was never a topic around our house. He was too proud, too determined, and one hell of a role model for an impressionable young kid, trying to figure out how to become a man. He handled his challenges so well that I almost thought that's what happened to everybody when they got older. As a kid, I remember wondering when I would grow up and be like him. I would ask him, "When do I get my crutches?"

If we went out as a family to a buffet somewhere that we had to stand up and walk around to get our food, he would give me a whack with his crutch if I ever tried to carry his plate for him. He was always so damned self-sufficient that it was just about impossible to help him with anything.

That was a unique and early lesson in perseverance for me. I learned not to let things hold me down and not to be afraid. As a result, I was fundamentally different from a lot of kids and adults as I got older, because I was always so comfortable with change. I knew that I had the perseverance to push through adversity, so change wasn't scary to me. My natural inclination was always to embrace adversity and seek opportunity in change.

I know I'm not the only one that was given powerful lessons early in life. Everyone should reach deep down inside them, and explore those strengths—whatever makes them special— as much as possible, and use it throughout their life.

Some of us have big personalities that break the ice easily

with certain crowds. Others are good at breaking down barriers to growth and paving the way for the team. Still others might be great at sticking to a calendar that provides near-guaranteed results. We all have strengths that can be leveraged to accomplish great things. It's just a matter of recognizing them and putting them to use.

Spot the Diamond in the Rough

McAfee had an unusual hiring practice, where incoming team leaders were interviewed by their potential direct reports. It was extremely awkward, and to be honest, I have no idea why they did it that way. I fail to see any value in it, and would never implement such a strategy. Nonetheless, one of the guys who interviewed me and later worked for me was Dave Hatchel.

Soon after coming on board, I recognized that Dave was very eclectic, meaning incredibly bright and emotionally charged. He was a super emotional guy, who could deeply connect with people very quickly, but he was full of quirkiness too. For instance, he was constantly spilling coffee on himself. He came to the office wearing nice clothes every day, but by noon, there was always a stain on his shirt from something.

Dave was an overall amazing guy, and someone people should want to work with, but he was misunderstood by so many of his peers. They had a hard time looking past his charged presence to get to the deeper levels of his prodigious talent.

Fortunately, one of my strengths is that I'm a good reader of people's strengths, so I didn't misunderstand Dave at all. I knew he was a diamond in the rough and how to leverage his strengths. So, I put him in positions where he could be the emotional leader for the team. If I got Dave on board with a project, I knew others would get behind it as well, because he was great at rallying the troops when we needed it.

Even if assessing people's strengths isn't something you're born with, you can still acquire that skill pretty easily. Consider the following three ways to do so.

1. **Assessments** – These tests help team members get better results by understanding their own motivations and those of others. Pull the team together and do a strengths assessment, like the Myers-Briggs test. Bring in an outside expert to conduct the test and explain what it means to each person.

2. **Sessions** – Another idea is to have people do the *Bury My Heart* sessions by Stan Slap, so they can start talking about things that shape them. People need a tool like that, because voicing those things doesn't come naturally to most of us. These kinds of sessions allow teams to get to know one another rapidly.

3. **People coaches** – You can also leverage people coaches, which are business coaches who specialize in the ability to pull forth true motivators.

These coaches will offer guidance and explain how to most effectively communicate with the different personalities on a team. They help you to understand unique qualities of various team members, so you can place them in the optimal positions for success.

It's not that hard, and I've seen people who were totally lacking in this skill make this formula work to achieve great team success.

Opportunity Knocks

While I was running my first team at McAfee in the West, another manager was running a team out East to somewhat of an infamous notoriety. To say that things weren't going well would be like saying the 2017 Cleveland Browns struggled en route to a winless NFL season. Whatever was going on there had turned so sour, that all of his employees had signed a joint letter stating that they would all quit if their manager wasn't fired.

The leadership team found themselves in a pretty unique situation with such an ultimatum, and they were desperately reaching for an idea of how to handle it. The first thing they did was they interviewed some of the team members to get a gauge for how serious they were about their collective threat. Evidently, the reps unanimously responded with a Teamsters Union type of attitude that leadership interpreted as very real and very serious.

So, the people in charge asked me what I thought about taking over the team. They said that I was one of the best "people managers" they had. They said, "What do you think about trying to solve this problem for us? We'll give you a raise." The job was supposed to be out of New York, but they said they would move me to Boston to be with my family.

At first, I wasn't interested at all, because there was a ton of risk involved. Surely, opportunity can come from a situation of dire need, but this seemed like an excessive situation of challenge even to someone like me, who is always looking for the next chance to grow my success.

The other reason it seemed so utterly unappealing was that I had grown to love the West Coast. I love my parents dearly, but I wasn't exactly amped about exchanging the warm California sunshine and laid-back aura of that area for harsh New England winters and the overcrowded hustle and bustle of Boston again. So, I politely reneged their first offer to bring me out there as a "fixer."

Undeterred from my initial resistance, they came back and told me that they were out of options, and wanted to know what I needed from them to take the job. I explained to them that my main goal was to attain VP status by age twenty-nine, and I was twenty-seven at the time, so ... They responded agreeably, "Well, if you're successful, we would be willing to sign up for that."

"Okay, then let's define success, shall we?" I said, "Because I don't want to go out there and execute a plan that I think of as successful, only to find out that I wasn't successful enough. I'll only do it if we can write up a contract that spells out how my success will be determined, complete with criteria and a reasonable timeline."

Next thing I knew, I signed on the dotted line and moved out to Boston.

I started in that setting like I always do, which is by implementing my process to align team strengths. After all, why would I waste my time trying to cram unsavory responsibilities and goals down the throats of people who already had a distaste for such a forced-feeding from management? Each team member read their results, so they had a clear understanding of how I think about people and some of the changes I wanted to make.

Then, I moved on to the typical process of breaking down complaints, things I need to fix, and things that were already working just fine. I explained to everyone my experiences of building a magical team and talked about our ideal endgame—the result we wanted to achieve together. I told them that we would need to earn our bargaining power, and it was going to take time. Rome wasn't built in a day and neither would our success. Regardless of how long it took, I explained that we were going to get there eventually, as long as everyone agreed to work together.

There was, however, an additional concern. Although the team came together to send a joint letter strong-arming leadership into making a change, they all kind of hated each other. Getting a team that knows little or nothing about each other to work together is one thing, but getting a team that actually *hates* each other, is a monumental task. My first goal was to figure out how to get this team to gel under these challenging circumstances.

The Carpenter's New England Bed and Breakfast

Each team member had their own set of quirks that made them stand out. Just like Dave was an emotional powerhouse and Craig was a scheduler-supreme, each of these reps had their "thing" too. One of them was an old-school Cuban guy named Orlando, who I grew quite fond of over time.

When I took over, Orlando hadn't missed his numbers in twenty-six quarters, but would tell people absolutely nothing when asked for a forecast. Like Fox Mulder from *The X-Files,* he trusted no one. He always anticipated 80 percent of plan, provided zero updates along the way, and delivered 100 percent.

At one point, Orlando had a meeting in Pennsylvania that I wanted to be involved with. The problem, of course, was that he had about as much interest in inviting me to the meeting as a rabid wolverine does in cuddle therapy. He didn't mind going with another rep, but he wanted no part of traveling with his boss and having me sit in on the meeting. So, I did what any good leader would do at that point—I forced my way in.

Here's where it gets a little weird. When our plane landed and we began checking in to the hotel, I found out that we were staying in the same room together.

I said, "Uhh, did someone make a mistake? What do you mean we're staying in the same room?"

Then he confesses, "I don't like staying alone in hotels."

This may sound strange enough coming from a grown-ass man of Orlando's age, but it was even more bizarre when actually watching the words come out of his mouth, because Orlando is a big muscular dude. I'm not sure what he was afraid of, but whoever decided to take on Orlando in a hotel room would need to either look like J.J. Watt or have some serious back-up. At first, I sort of scoffed at the notion for a second and laughed it off, because I was sure he was kidding, but he wasn't kidding.

Alas, I realized that I am nothing if not flexible, so I rolled with it. We went up to the room, unpacked our bags for a few minutes and decided to make the best of it by doing what most people do in an awkward situation like that: we went down to the bar and had a few drinks.

During the course of a couple drinks, we shared some stories, had some laughs, and the awkwardness began to slip away. Later on, I had the added pleasure of listening to him snore in my hotel room all night, so I guess that means we bonded, right?

At this point, I'm thinking that Orlando and I are good—we're tight. We drank together. He ruined my night's sleep by snoring like a chainsaw. No problems. I've officially won this guy over, because the trust has been built, and we're on our way to a productive relationship, right? Once again, Orlando surprised me with his resolve—scratch that, it was pig-headed stubbornness.

Two weeks later, I called him for a forecast, and he had the balls to give me the same line of bullshit he had given every other manager he had to that point—80 percent. My eyes just glazed over and my jaw held open for just a moment, as I realized that this guy still didn't trust me.

The next week I called him on the phone and said, "Hey, I want to go through your patch. I'm on the acquisition team, so I can't tell you anything that's happening from that aspect. But, if I can go through your patch, I can come up with an idea of how to set up your business and make you a lot more money. I know what's coming, and you have no idea."

That piqued his interest just enough to agree to let me into his business for a glance. So, I booked him a flight from New

Jersey to Boston as soon as I could. That's when I decided I was going to turn the tables on Orlando a little bit, and see how he reacted. If what I had planned didn't establish trust and get him on board as part of the team, then nothing would.

Unknowingly, he asked me where he should book the hotel, and I told him that I would take care of it.

When the time came for our meeting and his flight landed in Boston, I picked him up from the airport. We shook hands and exchanged some brief small talk before he asked me where we were going.

I answered, "Oh, we're going to my parents' house."

Confused, he asked, "Okay ... why are we going there?"

"Well, that's where we're staying," I said.

Finally, it started to sink in, and one more time for verification, he questioned me, "We're staying at your parents' house?"

"Yep." I answered. "I knew you had to stay with me, and my parents live here in Boston. If we're going to be in Boston anyway, I'm not going to a hotel, where you can keep me up all night with your snoring. We'll stay at my parents, where we can have our own rooms. If you want to get to know me, might as well know who I came from."

He just started laughing, and I think at that moment he realized that I wasn't going to just let him keep me at a safe distance—in his comfort zone—anymore. He was going to need to work with me and be part of the team, which was going to be a good thing for everyone.

We had a wonderful dinner with my parents, and he hung out for two days with the three of us. He learned everything about me: where I went to school, who my first girlfriend was, and some of the quirks that I had, just like he did—just like everybody does. From that point, I considered him one of my closest friends, and he told me everything about his business. As a matter of fact, that insight helped me set up a great quarter for him.

I had an idea I knew would fit his business. I couldn't share with him what I knew, but I knew the setup, the pricing structure, the quotas, and I left open areas to bundle new products in the pipeline. He didn't know what the new products were, and by the time the company bought the product, Orlando was prepped to execute the plan. He made $250,000 in commission his first quarter off the bundle X-factor I'd set up for the team.

My Time

My personal X-factor had been to get on that acquisition team to get early notice of what's coming and the ability to prepare within the limits of acquisition law. Trust was a major part of that, and it paid off. Not only did it help Orlando with his patch, but it also served as justification to get me to where I wanted to be. In other words, after I implemented this X-factor and got great results out of it, I checked that contract I signed with a promise to make me VP if I achieved a certain level of success, and wouldn't you know, I had accomplished what I needed.

After two years, I won RD of the Year, and showed top growth in the company worldwide. I met all the success criteria that leadership and I had previously defined, but then the bosses changed. That's not an unusual circumstance, because leadership always changes. Fortunately, I was always aware of that. I could tell that the new boss didn't take our agreement very seriously, but I was prepared, and I wasn't going to let him off the hook. After about six months, I started interviewing to shore up a Plan B.

I set up a meeting with him, his boss, and the head of North America when I explained, "Here's the deal: I did what I signed up to do for two years. I kept my end of the bargain, and I'm not going to live and die in this position, so I need to move."

They said, "Sure, we understand that. We'll get back to you in six months."

"No, I don't think you understand it at all then," I replied. "The agreement says now is when I should be moving up. If you don't do it in six weeks, I'll be leaving the company."

My next phone call was from Gene, the president of the

company at the time. He said, "Wait a second, you're not going anywhere. You're a rising star in this company, and I'm going to make this happen for you, but you're going to have to talk to Brian, who runs worldwide sales, and he'll get this done within six weeks."

Finally, they were taking this seriously. They came back with a few different VP options for me. One was in product marketing, another was something in Europe, and another one was to work for the federal vertical.

I looked at the position for vice president of fed. It was one of the smaller ones in the group, but I saw the growth potential. I could see right away a bunch of mistakes they had made in the business at a high level, so I knew there could be some easy wins there. I pursued it, and talked to the guy I would report to who gave me some references on the group.

Afterward, I called Brian and said, "Listen, none of those positions work for me."

He said, "What happened with the fed one? I thought you liked that one."

"Yeah, I interviewed for it," I explained. "But, the VP there—Frank—is beyond terrible."

"What do you mean he's terrible?" he said. "Frank is my guy. I brought him in here."

Although I knew that it may have slightly offended him, I didn't hold any punches and told him what I really thought. "His entire team hates him, because he's nothing more than a confrontational task master. He doesn't know anything about the business, doesn't get in front of the customers, and he has no personal skills. When he talks, it's just words with no meaning, or productive planning. He's a typical, status-quo, hard-headed, no-growth executive."

Brian stopped for a moment to take in everything I just told him, and said, "Well, what can I do to get you to take the role?"

"I don't want to have to report to that guy," I answered.

He told me, "Yeah, I know Frank can be a real pain in the ass, but I brought him in because there was a huge lack of detail in operations, and that's his strong point."

I said, "Yeah, I get that. But, I don't work well under people like that."

After thinking about it for a minute, he said, "What if I tell Frank that he's not to manage you like the others? Frank's worked for me for years at different companies." He sweetened the deal, "What if I also top that off with a $75,000 signing bonus?"

Still, I declined.

Not long after, Brian called me again and said, "I'm going to make sure that Frank doesn't screw with you, and you don't have the same problem that everybody else has with him." Then, Brian had Gene call me to validate and invite me to reach out to him if there was ever a problem, which would turn out to be key. The deal started to make more sense, and I finally agreed to take the role.

What usually happens when someone is warned to behave a little differently going forward is that they do exactly that for the short term. That's exactly what Frank did. For the first thirty days or so, he behaved himself. After that, not so much.

CHAPTER EIGHT

BE BULLY-PROOF AND BOLD

THE ROUTINE WHILE I HAD THAT ROLE AS VP OF FED BECAME for Frank and I to bark at each other like two dogs fighting over the same bone on a near daily basis. Soon after I started, the entire office knew that the two of us just couldn't co-exist.

With Friends Like This ...

One day, Frank instructed me to go talk to a "friend" of his. He said, "You need to talk to this guy. He's the best VP of fed that ever worked for me. In fact, he's forgotten more about fed then I've ever known. You need to ask him how to structure this system integrated (SI) group [blah, blah, blah]." Usually at this point I had stopped listening to him, but I heard the gist of it, and eventually I set up an appointment to meet with his friend.

The guy was the VP of fed at another Global 2000 software company, and he turned out to be a great guy. We sat down, and I began to get to the reason I was there by saying, "Hey, Frank is the one who gave me you as a reference. I'm new to the fed business and trying to figure out how to structure the SI team at McAfee. I'd love to hear your opinion on how you do it."

He started off with, "Frank told you to come see me?" He went on, " That motherfucker drug me through a mile of mud every fucking day! He is no doubt the worst boss I ever worked for in my life. You should run—don't walk—run away from him as fast as you can."

That rekindled my initial opinion that there was no way I wanted to work for that turd. So, in my head I was thinking, "Holy shit! This is his reference? If his friends talk about him like this, what did I get myself into here?"

Still trying to make the best of a bad situation, I went back to Frank after my meeting with his reference. I told him about the plan he gave me, the ideas we talked about, and how I needed to do things.

Most people would assume that it was a no-brainer that Frank would agree with the plan we came up with, because, after all, it was his reference who told me to do this. But, no, that's not the way Frank's brain worked.

Much to my surprise (although, nothing should have surprised me at that point), Frank said, "No, you're not going to do that."

I said, "Hold on, I thought you said this guy knew more about fed than anybody else."

"Fuck him," Frank barked, as sophisticated as always.

At that point, I was more than a little put off, so I responded, "Then, why the hell did you send me on a wild goose chase in the first place?"

Frank responded indignantly, "None of that matters. Here's the way you're going to do it."

I just looked at him as deadpanned as I could, and said, "No, actually that's not how I'm going to do it."

The end result of this goat rodeo was for a plan to be made on how the go-to-market for my vertical would be executed. Eventually, I sent the final draft of my plan via FedEx, along with a CD and digital records to Frank, his boss, and anyone else who had influence on the final decision. The ultimate result was Frank being furious with my final recommendation, and the executive team above and parallel to him, voting 100 percent with my final recommendations.

Exchanges like that were typical of how our dysfunctional relationship worked. They actually became somewhat legendary around the office for their entertainment value. As much fun as they may have been for everyone to talk about, those confrontations wore thin on me pretty quickly, and I started to look for any way I could to rectify the situation.

Bold or a Little Crazy?

Before my suffering subordination under Frank, another situation came up that proved to be somewhat of a milestone for me.

The president, Gene, and David (the EQ rep I mentioned earlier) came to me with a contract from a company named Siebel that we were doing business with. The contract had slipped through the cracks over the years, so that price increases were never applied since the days when McAfee was selling their product from a garage.

Siebel had only been paying us less than $30,000 per year for a contract that should have been worth around $250,000. Furthermore, there was no contractual obligation to hold the lower price; so they owed us a lot of money is the way I saw the situation.

Finally, we met with their executive team. We told them that their price was going up by about ten times, because they had been getting high-value features and functions for free over the last five years. We went on and explained that they had until the end of the month to renew.

Meanwhile, Siebel was trying to sell us a product to replace our existing CRM tool. Their sales team had been calling us a lot and was getting really pushy. So, they countered our proposal by telling us, "Yeah, we're not renewing anything unless you buy our new CRM product. If you don't, we'll just go to a competitor instead."

We responded, "Yeah, that's actually not how it works. See, we're both public companies, and even having a discussion about a deal like that could result in an SEC reporting violation if you plan on recognizing revenue from the transaction. I want to be on record as advising you not to have that discussion with us again, because we don't want any part of it." As most people would guess, that caused more than just a moment of awkward silence and some ruffling of feathers. But my response wasn't meant to throw the gauntlet down or to be any show of unnecessary bravado; it was a very functional statement. I wanted to set the record straight and make sure everybody knew that we were not going to be a part of anything illegal, and it was said with enough confidence to let them know that we were not going to be bullied.

After the air was cleared and everyone knew each other's bargaining positions, they responded with, "Okay, let's forget all that. Whatever the case, we're only willing to pay [x] dollars. (I forget the specific amount, but it wasn't close to the value they were getting out of the product.)

I replied, "Okay, you may want to have a back-up plan, as I wouldn't want your organization to take on any unintended risk based on the outcome of these discussions."

"What do you mean?" they asked. (As if they didn't know.)

"Let me make this clear," I stated. "What I mean is I'm going to shut you off at the end of the month, and no other security updates will be provided to the engines."

Getting defensive, they said, "Well, put that in writing then."

"No problem," I said, as I collected my papers, stood up, smiled politely, and let everyone know that the discussion was over.

So, I wrote a letter, stating very clearly that we were going to shut them off, the date it would happen, the price they would have to pay now, and the price they would have to pay later to reactivate.

Then, I set up a meeting with Gene, the president, so he could sign it. Gene read the letter and said, "Are you fucking crazy? This is Siebel you're talking about!"

"I know," I explained. "But, they've been using our product for next to nothing for ten years now, and they need to pay for it. Meanwhile, they're trying to sell us millions of dollars of their own product. Our cost is $250,000 a year for three years, that's $750,000, which, isn't that much money—not for Siebel."

His expression of restrained outrage didn't change much. "You do realize that if I send this letter, it could completely break off our relationship with them forever," he said.

I responded with barely a hesitation, "I understand."

Attempting to call my bluff, he asked, "So, what if I told you that if I sign this letter, and they don't renew it, you're fired?"

I told him, "Okay."

"You'd still have me sign this letter," he said, giving me one last chance to back down.

I took a deep breath to make sure I had a firm understanding of the situation, and ultimately responded, "Yeah, I feel pretty strongly about it."

He said, "Okay, I'll sign the letter. If they don't renew, you're fired." As he was telling me this, he was looking downward at the letter, while raising his eyes toward me as if he were a father about to trust his eighteen-year-old son with the keys to his Mercedes, mentally questioning him with something like, *"Son, are you sure you know what the hell you're doing?"*

Confidently, I replied, "Done deal. I'll take it."

"All right," he concluded, as he signed the letter.

Stunned silence, opened jaws, and slightly bulging eyes filled the conference room as Gene walked away. One person whispered behind his hand to me, "Holy fucking shit, Mike. What the fuck did you just do?"

I responded, "I guess I got him to sign the letter, right?" Then I attempted to show my conviction, but was probably only convincing myself at that point. I said, "Fuck yeah, they're going to sign the order. Of course, they are, right?"

And so, I sent Siebel the letter. I FedExed it, and sent it via email as well, just to make sure they got it. No sense in backing down now. Off went the letter that my future at McAfee rode on. I remained confident that this was going to work out, but Siebel sure did make me sweat.

It came down to the last day of the quarter. We had two hours left on their deadline and were waiting by the phone, biting our fingernails until they bled. As the last hour approached with still no deal in place, it was getting quite unsettling. "Should I update my resume and make some phone calls now?" I wondered.

Finally, I decided to go for a run to take my mind off of the ramifications that could be in front of me. I announced, "I'm not going to sit around here and sweat it out anymore as time expires." I grabbed the rep I was working with and we went for a forty-five-minute run. As I walked out the door, I said, "When we come back, you might be looking for a new boss, but at least we worked it out together. When it's all over, we can have a drink and relax."

We went off for our run and came back. I took a shower and walked upstairs to find Gene sitting in my office, waiting for me. For a moment, I thought to myself, "This is how it happens in the movies. The big moment comes and goes, somebody fails, and then, they find their boss waiting for them in their office just sitting there ready to lower the boom." Actually, if it was a gangster movie, it would be the mafia boss waiting in the form of Robert DeNiro or Marlon Brando, and after a really clever, but manly speech about honor and respect, I would be dead. So, treading carefully, I walked in, said nothing, and just waited. Gene got up out of the chair without a sound, ran to me, picked me up off my feet, and gave me the biggest man-hug in the history of the business world.

He screamed, "You were right! We got the order!"

After several moments of elation and shared celebration with the team, I began to think to myself, "I wonder if he really would have fired me?"

I thought about that for a while—several weeks, in fact—and I came to the determination that yeah, I think he would have fired me. Gene didn't know me very well yet. I hadn't proven anything to him. I was also a twenty-five-year-old hotshot, who looked more like a wet-behind-the-ears, nineteen-year-old. So, he probably would have lowered the boom, and thought he was teaching me a valuable lesson in the process.

The lesson I did learn from that, however, is that we can succeed by being bold. However, we need to be careful that we're not treading over the fine line of boldness to full-blown crazy. A little crazy can work sometimes, but it's definitely best to keep that to a minimum.

Who's Firing Whom?

My lessons with Siebel may have helped to prepare me for my experiences with Frank. In one of Frank's misguided discussions, he interjected with his periodic dose of mismanaged chaos and conflict. "Hey, I see you guys have been in there for a week now and established a full bid team there. Guess what? I read that RFP, and you're not going to win the business, so dismantle that team," he said, completely point blank and poker-faced.

Stunned for just a moment, because even for Frank, this was an exceptionally hasty, shortsighted, stupid thing to do. I started, "You have no idea what you're talking about. If I dismantle the ..."

He cut me off, "I've run fed for years. You don't know shit; just do it."

"This is a platform play," I said as I started to get frustrated. "If I lose this deal, our fed business is done. This is so critical I should have twice the number of people in there."

Steadfast in his stubbornness, he orders me, "No! Dismantle the team, and do it now."

Mostly because Frank left me no other choice, I called Gene from my office, and said, "This guy is driving me fucking crazy. I'll read you the bid, but if we lose this RFP, you can kiss goodbye to between seven and ten million bucks a year in fed. But, if we win, it's a hundred-million-dollar deal for us, and I'm not shitting you."

After I read him the deal, he determined, "Makes sense to me … do it."

I told him, "Then, you need to get my back, because he's going to come in and fire me." We hung up the phone, and then …

I heard the phone ring in Frank's office (which was right next to mine). Unwittingly as always, Frank answered on speaker phone for the entire office to hear Gene screaming at him, "Back the fuck off me!" With his tail tucked firmly between his legs, he hung up the phone and then came into my office.

"What the hell did you call Gene for?" he asked.

I said, "You're telling me to dismantle the bid team, which is the wrong thing to do. You were told that you're not allowed to try the same bullshit with me that everyone else lets you get away with."

He just stood there dumbfounded and said, "Well, I'm the boss. You can't talk to me like that, and you have to do what I say."

I responded, "I don't give a fuck who you are, and now I definitely plan on getting this bid complete."

After that, Frank realized that I wasn't backing down, and I had Gene's support to do it my way, so he just turned around and left without saying another word.

Eventually, I ended up winning the deal worth more than a hundred million dollars, and they fired Frank. Actually, his dismissal wasn't quite that directly related. The person Frank directly reported to (Brian), left. So, a new regime entered, and Frank's true colors shined through on his first meeting with them. Immediately, they pulled me aside and said, "We'll be back in a month, bear with us. He's going to be fired and we'll promote you."

All personal differences aside, Frank was pretty good at the operational aspect of the business. In other words, if precedent told him to push Lever A when Situation X happened, that's what Frank did. He never thought for a moment about growth, creativity, or planning on his own. His best move was the typical move of any manager stuck in a CYA mentality. He followed the people above him like a sad, but grateful puppy as a power play that he could leverage to bully the people around him into doing what he wanted.

Just in case anyone doubted his connectedness to the people that called the shots, he had pictures all over his office of him with his boss and other senior executives playing golf and going fishing. That way, whenever he pulled someone into his office for a meeting, those pictures served as extra intimidation for anyone that cared about that sort of thing, of which, I did not.

As far as leadership goes, Frank was terrible at it. He had no idea how to motivate people, no concept of teamwork, and served as a mountainous speed bump on the road to progress. The guy actually fired me twice.

The first time was after that meeting he had me attend with the former VP of fed. I was ready to pursue my own plan based on what his own reference told me to do, only to have Frank tell me to ignore it.

He called me upstairs one day and said, "That was a great quarter, but you're only at 95 percent of plan. I don't think that's going to cut it around here."

Totally prepared for something completely bonkers to come out of his mouth, I calmly responded, "True, but I have 400 percent growth and 95 percent plan, do you see a problem with that?"

He acted surprised, and said, "Well, if you don't like the plan, maybe it's time for you to quit."

I confronted him, "Frank, are you fucking firing me?"

"Sure am," he said.

Confidently, I replied, "Okay, good luck with that."

An hour later, the CEO called me and said, "Fuck Frank! He's not allowed to fire you."

Still a little pissed off, I said, "I want an apology."

"You'll have one in thirty minutes."

The Most Expensive Driver Ever

Not too long after that first firing from Frank, which was immediately rescinded, I was living in D.C. when my dad came down with ALS. I began a schedule of one week on, one week off work, so I could take care of my dad.

One day, while I was home, I got a call from Brian, who said, "Hey, Mike. I'm going to be in town next week, and I really want to meet with Lockheed Martin's CEO. Do you think you can set that up?"

"Sure, let me work on it, and I'll get back to you," I replied.

I secured that meeting within the next couple of days. Promptly after that, I called Brian and let him know that we were all set. He was pleased and told me to pick him up at the airport. I said, "No problem," and hung up.

On Sunday, which was one day before the meeting, Frank sent out an invitation for an internal team meeting that conflicted with the one I had set up for Brian and I with Lockheed Martin. So, I called Frank and said, "Hey, I saw your meeting invite, but I'm not going to be able to attend. Brian and I are meeting with Lockheed's CEO that day."

Frank responded, "Brian's in town? Why didn't you tell me?"

While sighing, because I could tell the conversation was about to take a bad turn, I said, "Yeah. It's not my job to tell you where Brian is and isn't. He said he was going to be in town for meetings. I figured you guys are best friends, so I was sure you already knew."

"No," he said. "He didn't tell me he was going to be in town."

I implored him, "Maybe you should talk to him then?"

Ignoring that, he just barked at me in his usual attempt at bullying, "You need to call me if an executive is coming to town."

I said, "Frank, I'm not the scheduler of our executives' comings and goings. That's somebody else's job, like an admin. If they want you to know they're in town, I'm sure they'll tell you."

With his ego bruised just a bit from the thought of being left out of an important meeting, Frank barked at me again, "You need to attend my meeting, and that's all there is to it."

"You're kidding me, right? You're going to make me miss a meeting with your boss's boss and a client's CEO to attend one of your one-hour conference weekly calls?" I asked as a passive question!

Frank reacted, "Look, you're going to have to learn to listen to me at some point."

"You're going to have to learn to stop trying to boss me around," I demanded, as I quickly ended the call.

Later, I picked up Brian at the airport. We headed to the meeting, and I said, "Hey, listen. This is a little bit awkward, but you told me that you would take care of Frank, and by the way, he is indeed a complete asshole, just as I expected."

He started laughing, as I continued, "He's not backing off, and he doesn't want me to go to this CEO meeting. Instead, he wants me to wait in the car and dial into his team call."

Brian asked me, "Is there something special or important about this team call?"

"No," I said. "It's going to be as useless as every other call that Frank has."

"You guys aren't getting along at all, eh?" he asked.

"No! He's a fucking asshole. I don't pull punches or usually talk negative to people, but he's impossible," I said.

Brian told me, "Then, you need to talk to him about this."

"I did talk to him about it, but he doesn't listen," I said. "The bottom line is, he wants me to sit in the car here. What do you want me to do?"

In a last-ditch attempt for a sane and reasonable resolution to the situation, I tried to call Frank one more time, but the team call had already started, and he didn't answer.

Brian said, "Let me call him." He left Frank a message that said, "Hey, I have the most expensive fucking limo driver I've ever had in my career, because that's what you told him to do … drive me to this meeting, instead of attending it, so he could be on your 'critical' team call. Call me back," and hung up.

Then Brian said to me, "Listen, I'm a guy who follows chain of command. If he said to stay in the car, do it, but I'm not happy about it, and I'll make sure Frank knows that later."

At that point, I lost complete respect for Brian, as well, because he enabled Frank's mismanagement. If that were me, I would have called him, fired him, and taken his former employee to the meeting, as I planned. That was a complete power play and full of disrespect, which has always been a major peeve of mine. People don't deserve to be treated like that, just because they're a subordinate. It's bad teamwork and bad leadership in action.

CHAPTER NINE

PLANNING FOR CAREER GROWTH

OPPORTUNITIES CAN PRESENT THEMSELVES IN BOTH BIG AND small companies. Whether you're looking to make the jump from rep to first-line manager or from manager to executive, the important thing to remember is to continue growing. Eventually, however, there's only so much growth to be had within a specific role, and that's when it's time to transition either the role or the company.

Identify the Sweet Spot for Change

As a rep, you get patches and quotas every year. Your job is to overachieve that quota, rinse and repeat the following year. The paradox, however, is that it becomes almost detrimental for you to keep busting your quota, because the more you do it, the higher (and more unreachable) your quota goes.

At some point, something needs to change, because sustained success requires consistent growth, and that's a key element of the inside-out approach. You can't afford to stand still, but there's only so much you can do after a few years of knocking your quota out of the park.

- You might be able to sell new products.

- You can get rid of some accounts that aren't buying, while allowing someone else to attempt breaking into them.

- Your quota could be lessened.

- Your territory could be split.

Territories can actually be split for years, all the way down to the point where you might only be selling to one account. But, even that isn't going to last forever. A lot of people get stuck in that spot. In my experience, three years in any position appears to be the sweet spot for change. That change could be as simple as splitting a territory, but if that's already been done to death, it might be time to look for that promotion or go to a different company.

Nobody should ever ask for a promotion during a down year, but if you're in a growing organization and achieving at a very high level, you should be presented with regular opportunities for growth. If not, you should be asking for them when the timing is right.

My career path was forged by striking while the iron was hot. Whenever I had a lot of success, I would make sure that leadership knew I was ready for my next role every two to four years. I suggest you follow a similar strategy.

It's a win-win situation anyway. I got the benefit of more success, and the organization reaped the rewards of my professional development. When they weren't able to provide me with the combination of professional growth and the ability for my efforts to create a material impact, I realized it was time to switch companies. If you find yourself outpacing the organization, that's when it's time to move on.

Does Size Really Matter?

I've worked for both small and large companies—a few years working at a smaller company, plus my time running my own businesses—and thirteen years working for larger organizations. I learned a lot along the way regarding the pros and cons of each, but I discovered that the key is to know what you're looking for.

Transitioning to Big Business

Bigger companies offer more structure, better boundaries, and a job that's already been defined and running. The company, the department, and the position have already been there for a long time, and chances are, no individual is going to impact it so much that any of that changes. Large organizations also provide the added benefits of mature technology and a value proposition. The customer awareness has already been done, and outreach is well underway. It's easier in some ways on the business side, because of all those business amenities. But the politics can be brutal and obstructive to progress.

When transitioning to a big business, I wish I had known about the politics first, because that awareness would have made things so much easier. I learned that in a bigger company, it's crucial to reach out to top leadership—the CEO, CFO, head of sales, and head of marketing—and analyze how they get along with each other. It's valuable to know what the corporate culture and the politics look like before you end up traversing some dangerous waters that you never intended to set sail on.

We went through a lot of different phases at McAfee with different CEOs. With each one, our culture completely changed. At a bigger company, you spend less time on the product and more time on politics with the leadership team. It's important to know who has backed them. How long have they been there? And what's the tenure of past leaders? As an experienced leader who has worked in the industry, I won't work for anybody that I don't know anymore. It's too hard, and it's too much risk to work for an unproven team that I know nothing about.

If you're a younger leader, you may not have that luxury, but you should still make sure to understand the average tenure of the leadership team. You need to understand the timeline of the last ten years. If the average tenure is four years, and the team is already at three and a half, that's not long enough for you to build a reputation with them.

I encourage younger salespeople and executives to work for the person, not the product, because good sales reps can find their way with any market-ready product. When looking at new companies, it's also important to realize that the leading products are not necessarily the best products.

For example, Cisco doesn't make the best firewalls or the best switches. They're the market leader, but they're not even close to being the best in my opinion. Also, McAfee and Symantec don't make the top five in their industry for overall product quality, but they're market leaders.

In business-to-consumer (B to C) dealings, product is more important. In B to B, the product may not have the most feature-rich solution, but the right team can definitely contribute to becoming the market leader, regardless of how good the product is. The whole package of networking, influence, pricing, branding, banking relationships, and vertical expertise are some of the leading drivers of what determines the market leader.

Transitioning to Smaller Companies

One of the biggest advantages of a smaller company is how agile they are. Because there is less obstruction to progress, they can naturally move a lot faster. Salespeople aren't turning a battleship in a bathtub in smaller companies. This easy maneuverability offers a lot of opportunity for creative minds and people who are willing to put forth the effort at inspiring real change.

Smaller companies also have fewer internal meetings, and they are more customer-facing. In the emerging technology sector, smaller businesses offer unique access into the executive teams of their customers.

I had better CIO access at a smaller company. Many rising CIOs are hungry to find technology that goes beyond the traditional models. They want to establish themselves as being on the cutting-edge and making an impact in their respective business. They look for advantages to take measured risks in areas that can have a material upside. That upside can include lower cost, faster route to value, and maybe even buying into a portfolio company of powerful venture firms. However, the CIO still needs that trusted relationship with the sales team and its executive leadership team. The CIO needs to ensure they fully understand everything that's happening, and remain aware of any risk they may be introducing to the business.

A meeting with the CIO might seem like a hurdle, but that challenge created opportunity for me. I built amazing executive-level relationships that will be part of my network forever. Above all, smaller companies afford you this golden opportunity to build a network of solid relationships that can last for your entire career. For that reason alone, smaller companies are certainly worth exploring in the earlier stages of anyone's career.

Smaller businesses lack the robust structure of larger organizations. The lines of organizational control are much more fluid, and the business needs to be guided by the salespeople. Therefore, there's a lot more grunt work involved. Some of the amenities you get at larger organizations like competitive intelligence organizations aren't going to be there. There won't be a lot of other resources to help with your internal blind spots or areas of weakness either. So, these roles naturally suit you better if you're more self-sufficient than the average person.

There definitely will be leadership issues and very likely issues with the founder at some point in a smaller company. A majority of founders aren't built to scale a company and don't have experience of leading large enterprises. They usually default to the disciplines they learned from inventing their product. They revert to these disciplines in a misguided effort to recreate the wheel for simple organizational tasks and structures. Founders of startups and small businesses don't necessarily hire great leadership or exude quality leadership either, because they've been overly concerned with the other key areas of business, like innovation and product launch. While big business will have more politics to wade through, it generally has more seasoned management and leadership to balance that struggle.

There's a better chance of making a big splash at a smaller company with a big payday included. However, there's usually a lower W-2 to count on as well. So, monetarily, there's a give and take.

If work/life balance is on the top of a salesperson's list, then I would say that a smaller company may not be the right fit. Smaller companies feed on hunger, outworking the big boys, and being on the go all the time. It's like one constant end-of-quarter push at most smaller companies, fighting to survive in the cold, shark-infested waters of the corporate world.

At the same time, smaller companies have fewer people muddying up the waters, which presents a great opportunity to differentiate yourself. Still, as they start to scale, they look externally for people with specific skills and more experience. In that regard, they create a double-edged sword, but there's still more opportunity for growth and freedom to move within the organization.

I'm not advocating for transitioning to bigger or smaller companies. Rather, I'm pointing out the differences that I've observed throughout my career. That way, you can make a decision based on whatever qualities you value the most. Some folks have a constant fire burning within them to create, innovate, and move forward. Others still want to do those things, but want to make sure they have enough time to enjoy family time and life at home. It's up to you to find the best opportunity that suits your individual needs.

Know What You're Getting Into

One startup I went to didn't work out. I thought we were aligned in creating a high-value company, built on the values of great leadership. Our plan included hiring the best of the best in every part of the organization and enabling them to blaze the revenue path of a very innovative product into the Global 2000.

What I didn't know was that I was building a family business—one that wasn't aligned with any core leadership values, unless you felt Hitler was a good role model for leadership. When the boss tells you he thinks he's a sociopath—run!

Littering your culture with anger and fear isn't something anyone should tolerate. The environment did not suit me at all, but I led a lot of great people to the company. Therefore, I felt a responsibility to be the best antidote to the poisonous bite of dysfunction.

A good lesson learned from this experience is that you should never sacrifice yourself if you made the wrong career choice. Make your exit fast and be willing to own a mistake in destination. To save myself and others a lot of anguish and hostility, I really should have conducted much better research in the first place.

Thoroughly researching companies and job prospects is absolute hell on Earth. It's boring, tedious, frustrating, and downright awful, but it's a necessary evil. Otherwise, you'll end up in an environment that sucks out loud, like the one I experienced. Likewise, if you do your homework, you can end up in a great situation, like the one I have now at CrowdStrike.

Do the Research

When considering a company move, it's utterly crucial to do the research. We've already discussed the importance of knowing the inherent differences between big and small companies. Now, it's time to discuss the process of properly vetting potential new employers with eight basic rules:

1. **Know the product from all angles** – Learn about the product from the customer's perspective, a partner's perspective, support, engineering—every angle you can think of. This helps to build a governing board that you can call upon to tell you what and where the company product is when you need it.

2. **Know the company's future goals** – Is it building toward an exit? Is an IPO in discussion? Do they want a balancer of power, or is it a family business? You need the answer, but unfortunately, the companies will lie to you. They'll tell you it's about the customer, which is a half-answer. Of course, it's about solving a problem. However, that's like saying I'm supposed to brush my teeth in the morning. No shit; but brushing my teeth isn't the main point of my day. The founders, however, will tell you that it's all about the customer and their

mission to protect or enable them. You, however, need to dig deeper than that.

You need to push them to find out what they really want. When considering the prospect of spending the next three years or more at an organization, leadership owes you the truth. You can't settle for corporate double-talk and accept a position with what amounts to blind faith.

Sometimes, I'd be very frank and say, "I know customers value your product or they wouldn't buy it, but what's your endgame? Do you want to be running this the rest of your life? Do you see yourself as a public CEO? If so, why do you think you can do it? If you want to sell it, who are the natural buyers along with your ideal goal and money for it? I understand things change, but what are you currently looking for?"

3. **Work with and interview board members** – It's important to remember, these are the people who are going to judge you without knowing anything about you.

   You need to know who the board members are, so you can attempt to have a relationship to leverage when you need it. The best way to create board value is to ask how you can use their contacts to help improve the business. Ideally, you want to be able to constructively talk with them to understand what their value is and what their expectations are for your contribution to the team.

4. **Figure out the culture** – First, determine what culture suits your needs best. For instance, do you prefer an office or a virtual work environment? Then, determine what the company is. Is it a financial culture, an innovation culture, etc.? In both big and small companies, it's important to align with one that matches your ideal culture. Are leaders empowered to make decisions? Is the company focused on "yes?" Or, does the company's version of empowerment end at "no?"

5. **Determine how personnel is viewed** – This is where you determine the value a company places on its people. All you need to do is ask, "As an organization, what's your biggest asset?" I ask that every place I go, and it's shocking to know how many executives start talking about their product.

It's the people that make an organization fly, not the product. People innovate ideas, persevere through challenges, and create solutions. An organization could have the greatest product in the world, but if it doesn't have the right people behind it, the company will fail. Align yourself with an organization that realizes the irrefutable value of its own talent.

6. **Examine the financials.** Financials are a look into the organization's health. The last company I worked for completely misled me on their financial position. I was told a story about how they both had founded a prior company and were independently wealthy. They went on to say that they never need funding, would be giving all proceeds to charity, and wouldn't take any VC funding. Unfortunately, I never verified any of it, which was a big mistake.

I was fortunate enough to have brought in a mainstream venture capitalist with me, and was the core ingredient to them raising $100 million in funding on their first formal round. That started the cycle of fundraising, which gave me the budget to scale the business. If that hadn't happened, there would have been a very different outcome, but I had no idea the risk they were taking in paying me. I wasn't cheap, and if I hadn't produced in six months, they would have had to fire me, because they lied about their private wealth, and I am confident they would not have been able to pay me for very long. The lies were endless; they even claimed they owned the building they were actually renting. They also talked about customer experiences that weren't true and clients they didn't have. In my opinion, it was fraud, but they got away with it.

Don't take anyone's word for anything, unless you're already very familiar with the situation as being trustworthy. Check out all the financials of an organization that you intend to work for, so there are no surprises down the road.

7. **Determine departure terms upfront** – Be a stickler on this. These details seemed generally irrelevant to me at one time. I thought if it didn't work out, I would find my way out of it somehow. The laws have changed, and that's not so easy anymore.

8. **Inspect the backers** – Research into the company's majority stockholders. It doesn't matter if they're the founders or a bunch of venture capitalists. In my second season of growing a small company, I profiled VCs, so I knew which ones I would and wouldn't work for.

There was one VC with which I had a great relationship. It was top ten in the valley with an elite, multibillion-dollar investment portfolio. But I wouldn't work for them, because I saw a disturbing pattern. Right before they launched an IPO for a company, they ousted the head of sales. When I turned down their respective offers, I let them know why. They said it wasn't true, but then I started naming companies.

Finally, I made them realize what they were doing.

"You guys don't even realize you're doing it," I told them. "You're taking out class-A players and replacing them with class-C players before an IPO."

They were blown away, because it was the first time they had ever heard that. They turned to me somewhat sheepishly, and said, "You're absolutely right."

"I would change it," I said.

They offered, "How about we change it together?"

"No, no, no, no." I just came out of three years of hell, and I'm not signing up for that again anytime soon.

The Startup

When I was very young, I started my own small business with about sixty people working in it. I loved flexing my strengths, making big decisions, and exercising entrepreneurial freedom. There was also something very appealing to me about working with a blank canvass. My partner and I shared a crystal-clear vision of the product, and it was really exciting to build our own culture and our own team, while being in charge of our own destiny. But those advantages didn't come without a cost. There were struggles too.

From a personal perspective, I struggled to strike a healthy work/life balance, which is somewhat more manageable as a twenty-something with no spouse, kids, or house to maintain, but certainly not ideal for someone with different responsibilities to consider. Making it more difficult, I lived with the cofounder, so we worked morning, noon, and night. There was no downtime. I also lacked a solid grasp of the operational requirements for scaling. I didn't really know which systems were available and what to leverage as we grew.

From an operational perspective, a big downside was how hard it was to manage when business took a hit from an unforeseen obstacle.

Black Friday

At one point, we had raised and/or committed roughly $9 million, when a *Barron's* article broke the story about startup burn rates and all the companies that were about to go out of business. It single-handedly eviscerated the VC market, which was very bad for business.

Everyone was frantic. It felt like the historic stories of Black Friday, as investors from all over were calling us. Some of them had already been smoked on other investments earlier in the day, so they were all trying to get their money back from anything that wasn't fully guaranteed.

The result was that we lost some funding commitments. From there, the pressure to immediately get into a cash-flow-positive position was on, because the board demanded it. That's when we had to do one of the hardest things I've ever had to do in my lifetime, which was to cut thirty people overnight—most of them were damned good employees too, and people with real commitments and responsibilities.

D-Day

The day of the cut is the most painstaking day for me to reflect on in my entrepreneurial endeavors. I had to witness all those people who were feeling successful get sent back to their families and friends jobless, because we couldn't afford to keep them.

After that day of orchestrating the departures, I literally locked myself in my office for hours. It crushed me to let those people go, and I felt what they were feeling. I wouldn't have known what to say or what to do in their position. Other than a meaningless job at a bagel shop when I was very young, I had never been fired in my life.

I was thinking of the disappointment and shame of having to go home and say, "I wasn't good enough to keep." There was a selection process, and some just didn't make the cut for whatever reason existed.

That was my hardest day. Thirty people gone out of sixty made the office look, sound, and feel empty. That day motivated me to make sure I was ahead of that game going forward, and I could control the outcome if I made a commitment to people for their success. The worst part was that I didn't foresee D-Day ever happening. I hadn't factored that into my commitments to people.

One of the things that I didn't realize then but I've come to realize now is that the business is a mirror of the leaders—the CEOs, the founders, and even into the executive team—and the brand is associated with them. When employees get mad at the company, they're mad at the leader.

Nobody had a shortage of words to rip into us on their way out the door, and I don't blame them even 1 percent for feeling that way. I agreed that the responsibility fell on us, but there wasn't anything more I could do about it either.

People Come First

Founders need to consider and care about the people they take with them when they start a business. Unfortunately, most of them don't.

Between my experience at McAfee and my current role at CrowdStrike, I spent almost three years working at a smaller company, which was a horrible experience. The mistake I made there was that my desire to be a people pleaser and trying to make things work took over. It pisses me off when I think about what happened there. I would never have allowed that to happen anywhere else in my career.

It all started well enough. When I entered the business, it had no salespeople, and was operating with very little revenue. Three years later, we brought that up to an estimated $3.75 billion valuation. The company was off and running. Normally, that level of success would be great, but in this case, the founder was a self-described sociopath. Believe me, in startups, that's not as uncommon as most people think.

Startup entrepreneurs are a unique breed. In my case, as the CEO became more successful, he seemed to become less concerned about the people that led him to his initial success. What was tolerable to me in the beginning became sickening toward the end. He treated employees terribly, and I watched it go much further than it should have.

I built tons of great relationships while I was at that company, but I felt that the founder took advantage of them at every turn—from employees, to partners, and even personal relationships. The way it broke down was, I built up a relationship, and he tore it down. Eventually, the rampant destruction of relationships became too much for me to handle.

Finally, I brought all of my concerns to the founder and told him, "You need to fix it, sell the company, or find a new head of sales." One week later, I was fired.

Adding insult to injury, he also falsely told people in the industry that I was obssesively abusing illegal drugs and tried to prevent me from gaining further employment.

Fortunately for me, his efforts had limited industry impact, because my past successes preserved my reputation.

I originally planned to take some time and heal from the

tortures of working for some really bad people. I figured I would ski, work out, eat right, and get some additional quality time with my amazing children. That all changed after my first VC meeting. Out of the blue, they started asking me about illegal drug abuse that was responsible for poor business results. So much for the mental health benefits of a sabbatical. I had to get out in front of the rumors, and let potential investors and employers look me in the eye and view the clean lab work for themselves. It was very embarrassing, but as leaders, we need to be resilient to business bullies that let their egos run amok. I met with every single VC and business leader I knew and countered the rumors with truth.

The lack of integrity engrained in this founder continues to harm present and past employees to this day. Most companies try to keep their 409A valuation level low for common stock value, as it creates a larger tax obligation for employees as it increases. This founder bragged about being able to muddy the process, so that employees who earned stock couldn't leave and afford to buy their stock due to the tax implications. He wanted leverage with the ability to punish those who chose a different path. If they left the company, they typically reclaimed the stock value created by their efforts as a result of the increased tax burden. Unfortunately, the issues of integrity didn't stop with harming employees.

As reported in Bloomberg, for years, the CEO made high-level presentations to CIOs and security officers using live data of one of the company's active clients without their knowledge or permission. Sometimes, the client would not be revealed, but other times a specific query would be demonstrated at audience member request and reveal granular information, like the names of the most vulnerable machines in the client's network. Bloomberg quoted David Appleman, law partner at Montgomery & Hansen LLP:

> "By revealing weaknesses in El Camino Hospital's IT architecture, Tanium may have violated federal and California state laws, including the Computer Fraud and Abuse Act and the California Comprehensive Computer Data Access and Fraud Act ... Certainly, it's bad business practice ... It sounds insane."

Today, I'm fortunate enough that the founder I'm working for at CrowdStrike cares about his people a lot. In fact, that's one of the reasons I selected them. I worked with him for years at McAfee, but I hadn't seen quite the degree of care that he had for people until recently.

I was at a club event in Hawaii. One of the first salespeople at CrowdStrike had recently passed away, and George—the CEO and founder, who had been having a great time until then—suddenly got up to give a toast and a moment of silence. I saw the supreme sadness in his eyes that overtook him for a moment, and he remained subdued for the rest of the night. It seemed like he was replaying every conversation he had in the past with this man. He was obviously feeling the pain of the man's family and those who loved and missed him.

To me, that degree of genuine care for people is more power-ful than anything else. It makes me get up early to work the next day. Knowing that the boss cares that much about the people around him is a corporate value that most of us can really align with.

A lot of people try to fake that sort of caring and consid-eration, but usually it wreaks of disingenuous intent and smarmy pseudo-altruism. We can smell it when they walk in the room. It seeps through the perspiration on their hands as they shake ours to greet us. And, it leaves an aura of ugli-ness in their wake. I've seen that too. People fake their value systems to their own advantage, but it's easy enough to spot if you're paying attention.

People are first. They make things happen, and an organiza-tion that holds its people as its biggest asset, is capable of very powerful things.

CHAPTER TEN

LEADER OF THE PACK

I OWE MOST OF MY SUCCESS TO KNOWING HOW AND WHEN to break the rules and not being afraid to try new ideas. That approach was the biggest factor in empowering me to compete and succeed like a true sales leader. Hard work was never a problem for me and neither was perseverance or creativity. I'm willing to bet those things aren't a problem for you either. But, my unique approach probably made the biggest difference for me, and it can work for you too.

- Don't just go through the motions, because that's the way things have always been done. Think outside the box for solutions and question status-quo activities.

- Don't allow career or company growth to get bogged down by being incorrectly focused on the CYA mentality. Challenge that by remaining accountable and sharing responsibility and accountability for wins and failures.

- Place the utmost emphasis on teamwork. Only with the collaboration and recognition of hardworking people around you can you truly rise to the top of anything.

As a rep, you advance by surpassing goals and expectations as an individual. You get upset when products don't measure up, and your instinct might be to immediately shift blame. An inside-out shift from CYA as a rep to teamwork, revolutionizes the whole culture of the team. As you advance to management and eventually executive leadership, that inside-out shift has the ability to evolve the culture of the entire organization.

The Difference Altruistic Leadership Can Make

When I was at McAfee, I had multiple CEOs and leaders running big chunks of the business who had very different views.

Joe Sexton taught me a lot about altruism and its place in corporate America. Originally, he was set to coauthor this book with me, because he was one of the most altruistic leaders I had ever worked for. He became a positive mirror for his organization, and the people started to come together around his leadership and communicate more effectively.

Everyone held themselves more accountable under his leadership. Those who didn't take all the credit for the wins were rewarded with movement in their career. Those who didn't oblige weren't necessarily terminated, but they weren't recognized for the success of leadership growth.

Just like a bad seed can grow like a weed in an organization, so can a good one. We had multiple CEOs above Joe, and the culture changed with every one of them. The biggest positive impact was with Dave Dewalt.

His leadership wasn't just a message about commanding down from the top. It was about getting in the field, listening to the customers, understanding the product value, setting a vision, reaching down and moving out disruptors, and bringing in people who had the right values to grow the business. Dave was a great leader and did a phenomenal job of bringing in the right cast of characters. Everybody was very different, but he was able to take that very diverse group, play to their strengths, bring them together, and flourish.

Before Dave got there, the leadership had gone through periods of extreme weakness. The CFO, the CMO, and the general counsel all had become highly competitive with each other. They symbolized the CYA mentality, because they constantly acted as individual contributors and blamed each other for failures.

The degradation was fascinating and terrible at the same time. From the CEO down, everybody was fighting to be recognized and blaming others for failure. It spread like cancer through the organization until it peaked. The CEO was removed, and they brought in Dave.

Immediately, Dave made the corrections. He brought in new leaders like Mike DeCesare, for worldwide sales, and made an immediate impact. Mike was an operational genius, who also had an eye for elite sales talent. He focused on the top players and built an unbreakable loyalty with them. If you made Mike's list of high-potential employees, your career was about to take flight. His operational lessons continue to be the key ingredient with many of the disciples he trained across the software industry.

Dave's team gave employees a place to look up to and emulate. He led by example and didn't just sit in an office and make decisions by the seat of his pants. He was incredibly active with customers, listening, changing directions, and setting courses. It was no longer about who wins; it was about everybody winning—together.

A prior CEO promised to shave his head if the company stock achieved a certain value. The next tier down in value meant he'd wear an earring. I imagine the sycophants below him were cheering on this idea, but this was not about winning as a team. It was entirely self-focused. Of course, the story then becomes about the CEO's amazing turnaround, and he grabbed the front-page cover of a magazine. That misplaced focus was precisely where the breakdown started though.

People should have stood up and said, "You know what? This is everybody's win. This is about putting customers first and holding ourselves accountable. It should be about creating a place where people want to work, not grandstanding displays of misplaced individual focus."

So much of corporate success comes down to leadership and the ability to pull the group together to shift the organization's culture. When a shift to positive leadership happens, like when Dave and his team took over, it's unbelievably rewarding to watch.

My Leadership Evolution

I've tried to take with me as many of the lessons about leadership from Joe, Dave, and Mike as I could. I'm no longer the young gun or the rising star, but I definitely have more leadership responsibilities than I had in those days.

Growing up through the business, I was always the youngest in my role. Most people looked at my age and said, "Wow, that must have been hard to overcome." But I looked at it as a major advantage, because it made me unique and memorable. It was something to talk about, and the fact that I could use it as a disarming tactic was a powerful tool for me. People would expect a lower level of professionalism based on how I looked, and they would witness an unexpectedly higher level when I started making changes. So, I had the element of surprise working well for me in those days.

As my career evolved, I lost most of that element of surprise, because after a while, people's expectations changed. They were no longer surprised by any of the changes I made or the successes my teams had. Therefore, my skill set had to evolve along with my experience. As I rose through the ranks, different skills became necessary to continue growth. The same evolution will need to take place for you, if you follow a similar path.

Along with the growth in my career responsibilities has come a shift as a leader. Today, my position is less about tactical execution, and more about planning, talent recruitment, and culture management. It's not about closing the big deal or forcing a change in the business anymore. Rather, I strive to ensure that the right people are engaged in the right activities. It's about allowing them to have fun, while succeeding in their roles, because I've put them in a position to win.

Ultimately, my goal is to have the same culture of trust, both internally and externally. The biggest responsibility I have as a leader today is to nurture both relationships through transparency, so everybody knows what my motivation and the logic behind my decision-making is at all times.

The Importance of Self-Investment

I believe wholeheartedly in spending the necessary resources to invest in myself, which is why I hire a personal coach to advise me every other year. Together, we work on methodologies and adjustments for the following year. Every other year is a great cycle for me, because constant coaching would not allow me to see and measure the impact of changes.

The year of coaching starts with understanding, then identification of weaknesses, and the implementation of tailored techniques. The following year is the proving ground, where I evaluate my performance and decide if that same coach is still the right one for me.

Different coaches work well for different people. Once again calling on a sports reference, think about it from a football perspective. Some players respond well to the totalitarianism of a Bill Parcells type of head coach, where he's going to get in a guy's face, call his mother a bunch of nasty names, and tell him to run fifty laps after doing a thousand push-ups, just to see if it properly motivates him to pay attention a little more when he's talking about the game plan. Meanwhile, other players respond better to the footloose and fancy-free style of Pete Carroll, where he's "pumped and jacked" about everything football. He might even break out a cheerleader costume and waive some pom-poms around if that does it for the guy. We can scoff at it all we want, but both methodologies win. Both coaches have Super Bowl titles under their belts. The same goes for sales, and the same goes for sales coaches.

One company had a coach they assigned to a bunch of us on a team. This coach had a great ability to deal with people. She was awesome at helping leaders show their true selves to their employees and relate in difficult conversations to resolve conflict. The problem was that those were exactly the same things I would identify as strengths for myself. In fact, I should have probably been right there by her side, helping her get her point across, because her approach just happened to mirror my natural skill set. Therefore, there wasn't much value in me speaking with her.

Finally, I had to tell my boss, "Hey, this isn't working for me. The coach is absolutely fantastic, but her methods don't address any of my weaknesses. Most of the things she talks about are already strengths of mine." He said, "Holy crap, you're exactly right." That kicked off a program where coaches were matched to different leaders based on individual strengths and weaknesses. If something isn't a fit, it's very important to speak up and let it be known.

CHAPTER ELEVEN

KEY TAKEAWAYS

I THINK THERE'S A FAILURE IN THE WAY THE SALES INDUSTRY currently trains and recruits its leaders. We learn to sell before we learn to lead. The following is a breakdown of the key takeaways from each chapter to take with you on your own path to sales leadership.

CHAPTER ONE: The Road Less Traveled

- True leaders don't just stay out of the way. The "stay out of the way" sales manager performs all the administrative tasks to let their best reps sell, while trying to help their weaker reps make quotas. It's akin to an overpriced administrative assistant.

- True leaders also don't just become super reps. This is a common occurrence when the best performing reps get promoted to management. They know how to sell the hell out of anything, but not necessarily how to lead people.

- Successful sales performance starts with teamwork. Encourage all team members to work with each other, rather than against each other.

CHAPTER TWO: Stop Doing It Wrong

- Be bully-proof. Don't let team members or cow-orkers strong-arm their way into easy quotas or underperformance.

- Bigger quotas or territories don't always mean bigger success. Sometimes fewer accounts can translate to knocking a reduced quota out of the park, rather than spreading a rep's territory too thin and leaving a lot of sales untapped.

- If a salesperson is failing because they just don't have the necessary skill set, let them go right away. It will be better for both of you in the long run.

CHAPTER THREE: Planning for Success

- Plan your actions, while always considering future variables. Think like a chess master or a pool shark who thinks several plays or shots ahead of the one they're making.

- Reps can thrive by being a slave to process. Leaders, however, need to remain flexible and change course when needed.

- Natural sales ability isn't everything. Many times introverts who are driven and well prepared can outperform "natural" salespeople.

CHAPTER FOUR: Stop Covering Your Ass

- Be bold; don't just cover your ass by camouflaging weak spots. Create ways to improve and increase business.

- Make yourself the easy win for upper management by building mutual trust with colleagues organization-wide.

- Transform problems into opportunities by handling service issues so efficiently that the customer actually wants to increase their business.

- Don't waste your time by doing paperwork that nobody reads or cares about.

CHAPTER FIVE: Bring in the Boss

- Don't be afraid to call upon the CEO to close a deal if it will make a difference.

- Get other departments on your side, such as engineering, finance, and support by being transparent and building a relationship based on trust.

CHAPTER SIX: More Than Success

- Know the difference between managing and leading. Managers manipulate, control, and provide administration. Leaders plan a path for achievement or success, while enabling others to succeed.

- Most salespeople should plan to change roles every three to five years for sustained success. Staying in a role too long allows too much comfort, which stunts growth. Keep moving forward, while building new relationships and achieving new success.

CHAPTER SEVEN: Manager Material

- Ego needs to grow with your career. You need to believe in yourself and understand that you are entirely capable of over-performing in your new set of responsibilities with each role or promotion.

- Don't, however, let your ego run amok. Treat people with mutual respect, no matter what role they have within your organization or outside in your personal life.

- Identify key strengths and weaknesses in your own skill set, as well as in others. Then, leverage those strengths accordingly. Consequently, if someone is particularly weak in one area, don't ask them to fulfill that role. Creatively find ways around forcing them to do something they're not good at.

- Always be looking for the diamond in the rough. Just because a person is struggling, doesn't mean that they're not capable of the job. Find out if they have something that makes them special, and see if they can leverage that one unique trait to succeed.

CHAPTER EIGHT: Be Bully-Proof and Bold

- Know the difference between bold and crazy. Don't be afraid to take a calculated risk every so often, but don't do anything so risky that it doesn't make sense.

CHAPTER NINE: Planning for Career Growth

- Big businesses offer more structure, better boundaries, and roles that are already defined and running. The politics, however, can be difficult to manage.

- Smaller companies are more agile, have fewer internal meetings, and are much more customer-facing. The disadvantages are that there is a lack of structure and leadership may have too much power.

- Whenever transitioning your role into a bigger or smaller company, always perform due diligence and perform exhaustive research before making a decision on a new company or role.

CHAPTER TEN: Leader of the Pack

- Altruism has a big place in strong leadership. Beware of the selfish leader who accepts too much credit when things go right, and not enough blame when things go wrong.

- Self-investment is important. Accept coaching and consistently work on new methodologies.

CONCLUSION

I WAS HONEST WITH MYSELF, AND I THINK THAT MAY HAVE been the biggest reason for my sustained success. There were plenty of challenges along my road less traveled to success. I worked for and with some awful people—tyrants, bullies, and maybe even sociopaths. But, I also worked for some amazingly talented, determined, and strong people striving to make things better for everyone around them, including themselves.

Sustained success is within your grasp too, but you need to start thinking differently to make it happen. Take a fresh perspective, try some new ideas, and don't be afraid to break the rules when the time is right. That is the path to true sales leadership.

Made in the USA
Middletown, DE
04 March 2018